I0479096

# INVESTING LEGENDS

*The Proven Strategies of Value, Growth, and Momentum Investing*

*JACK FISHER*

**Copyright © 2023 by Jack Fisher. All Right Reserved.**

No part of this publication may be reproduced, distributed, or transmitted in any form or by any means, including photocopying, recording, or other electronic or mechanical methods, or by any information storage and retrieval system without the prior written permission of the publisher, except in the case of very brief quotations embodied in critical reviews and certain other noncommercial uses permitted by copyright law.

Limit of Liability/Disclaimer of Warranty: While the publisher and author have used their best efforts in preparing this book, they make no representations or warranties with respect to the accuracy or completeness of the contents of this book and specifically disclaim any implied warranties of merchantability or fitness for a particular purpose. No warranty may be created or extended by sales representatives or written sales materials. The advice and strategies contained herein may not be suitable for your situation. You should consult with a professional where appropriate. Neither the publisher nor author shall be liable for any loss of profit or any other commercial damages, including but not limited to special, incidental, consequential, or other damages.

Table of Contents

# PART 1.
# INTRODUCTION
# TO INVESTING

*"Successful investing is about managing risk, not avoiding it. It's about achieving balance, not chasing returns. And it's about focusing on the long-term, not getting caught up in short-term market fluctuations. Investing can be both rewarding and challenging, but the key is to approach it with a clear understanding of your goals, your risk tolerance, and your investment time horizon. With the right knowledge and mindset, anyone can become a successful investor, regardless of their background or experience."*

*Janet Yellen*

# CHAPTER 1. AN OVERVIEW OF INVESTING

Investing is the act of allocating money or resources with the expectation of generating profit or returns in the future. The concept of investing is as old as human civilization, as people have always sought ways to grow and preserve their wealth. In today's world, investing has become a fundamental aspect of personal finance and a tool for achieving long-term financial goals. There are many types of investments available, each with its own unique characteristics and risks. Some of the most common types of investments are:

1. Stocks: Shares of ownership in a company. When you purchase stocks, you become a part-owner of the company and are entitled to a portion of its profits. Stocks are considered a high-risk investment, as the value of the shares can fluctuate rapidly.

2. Bonds: A type of loan that investors make to corporations, governments, or other entities. When you purchase a bond, you are essentially lending money to the issuer, who promises to pay you back with interest at a future date. Bonds are generally considered a lower-risk investment than stocks, but they also offer lower potential returns.

3. Real Estate: Involves buying and managing properties, such as rental units or commercial buildings. Real estate is generally considered a long-term investment, as it can take time to generate significant returns. However, it can also be a high-risk investment, as property values can fluctuate rapidly.

4. Mutual Funds: Investment vehicles that pool money from multiple investors to purchase a diversified portfolio of stocks, bonds, or other securities. Mutual funds are considered a lower-risk investment than individual stocks, as they provide diversification across multiple companies and industries.

5. Exchange-Traded Funds (ETFs): Similar to mutual funds, but they are traded like stocks on an exchange. ETFs provide investors with the ability to purchase a diversified portfolio of stocks or bonds in a single trade.

Investing is a vast and complex world, with many different strategies and approaches that investors can use to build their portfolios. Three of the most popular investing strategies are value investing, growth investing, and momentum investing. Each of these strategies has its own unique characteristics and can provide investors with a different set of potential rewards and risks. In this chapter, we will explore these three investing strategies in more detail, providing an overview of what they are, how they work, and the types of investors who may be most suited to each approach. Whether you're a seasoned investor or just starting out, understanding these different approaches to investing can help you make more informed investment decisions and achieve your long-term financial goals.

Value investing is an investment strategy that seeks to find undervalued companies and purchase their shares at a discount to their intrinsic value. The idea behind value investing is that by purchasing stocks at a discount to their true worth, investors can reduce their risk and potentially earn higher returns over the long term.

Investors who follow the value investing strategy tend to search for businesses that are priced below their book value, earnings, or cash flow. Such investors prioritize companies with robust fundamentals, including a strong history of earnings growth, a healthy balance sheet, and a competitive position within their industry. Furthermore, these investors seek out businesses that offer a margin of safety, allowing them to buy shares at a substantial discount to their intrinsic value, which helps to safeguard against potential downside risks.

One of the most famous value investors of all time is Warren Buffett, who built his fortune by following a value investing strategy. Buffett believes in the importance of purchasing great companies at a discount, and he looks for companies with a strong competitive advantage, solid earnings growth, and a history of generating free cash flow.

One of the key principles of value investing is patience. Value investors are willing to wait for the market to recognize the true value of a stock, even if it takes years for that to happen. This approach requires discipline and a long-term focus, as value stocks may not perform well in the short term but can be rewarding over the long haul.

Growth investing is an investment strategy that focuses on investing in companies with high growth potential. The idea behind growth investing is that by investing in companies that are growing rapidly, investors can potentially earn higher returns than the overall market. Growth investors typically look for companies with strong earnings growth, a strong competitive position in their industry, and a track record of innovation and investment in research and development.

Investors who prioritize growth tend to focus on businesses that hold a dominant position within their industry and are in the process of expanding their market share. They specifically seek out companies that are innovating and disrupting their industry, often by creating new markets. Although such companies may not have an extensive history of profitability, their potential for growth is the primary factor that draws investors towards them.

Investing in companies with a long-term growth outlook is a fundamental aspect of growth investing. Such companies may not generate substantial earnings or dividends in the short term, but their potential for growth is what draws investors towards them. Growth investors generally have a longer investment horizon compared to value investors and are typically more tolerant of higher levels of volatility, as they aim to achieve higher returns over time.

Another important aspect of growth investing is diversification. Growth investors typically hold a portfolio of stocks across multiple industries to reduce the risk of any single stock or industry having an outsized impact on their overall portfolio performance.

One of the most famous growth investors of all time is Peter Lynch, who achieved remarkable success during his tenure as the manager of the Fidelity Magellan Fund. Lynch focused on investing in companies with strong growth potential and was known for his willingness to invest in companies outside of his area of expertise.

Momentum investing is an investment strategy that seeks to capitalize on the tendency of stocks that have performed well in the past to continue to perform well in the future. The idea behind momentum investing is that stocks that have exhibited strong price trends in the past are likely to continue to exhibit strong price trends in the future.

Investors who prioritize momentum tend to search for stocks that have demonstrated robust price trends over the preceding six to twelve months. These investors specifically seek out companies that display positive momentum, which implies that their stock price has been consistently increasing over time. Additionally, such investors may also examine other factors that point towards positive momentum, including a company's revenue growth, earnings growth, or market share.

One of the key principles of momentum investing is to invest in companies with positive price momentum and to sell companies with negative price momentum. Momentum investors may also use technical analysis to identify trends in the stock market and to make investment decisions based on those trends.

The application of momentum investing is not limited to a particular asset class and can be extended to various assets, including stocks, bonds, or commodities. Moreover, momentum investing can be applied to different regions and markets.

One of the advantages of momentum investing is that it can provide high returns over a relatively short period of time. However, momentum investing can also be risky, as stocks that have exhibited strong price trends in the past may not continue to exhibit strong price trends in the future. In addition, momentum investing can be affected by market volatility, and momentum investors may experience significant losses during market downturns.

Another potential disadvantage of momentum investing is that it can lead to overvalued stocks. If too many investors are investing in a particular stock based on its positive momentum, the stock price may become overvalued relative to its intrinsic value.

# PART 2.
# FUNDAMENTAL
# ANALYSIS

*"Fundamental analysis is the bedrock of investing. The process of studying and evaluating the financial health and performance of a company, industry, or economy provides a solid foundation for making sound investment decisions. It requires discipline, patience, and a willingness to dig deep into the data to uncover the true value and potential of an asset."*

*John C. Bogle*

# CHAPTER 2.
# ANALYZING FINANCIAL STATEMENTS AND OTHER KEY METRICS

Analyzing a financial statement is an important skill for investors seeking to make sound investment decisions. Proper analysis involves examining a company's balance sheet, income statement, and cash flow statement to evaluate its financial health and stability. However, there are common pitfalls to avoid when conducting financial statement analysis.

To properly analyze a financial statement, start by examining the balance sheet. The balance sheet provides a snapshot of a company's financial position at a specific point in time. It lists the company's assets, liabilities, and equity. Analyze the balance sheet to understand a company's financial strength and stability. Here are the main parameters to look for in a balance sheet analysis:

1. Current Assets: Current assets are assets that can be converted into cash within one year. Examples include cash and cash equivalents, accounts receivable, and inventory. Analyze trends in current assets to understand a company's liquidity.

2. Non-Current Assets: Non-current assets are assets that cannot be easily converted into cash and have a

useful life of more than one year. Examples include property, plant, and equipment, and intangible assets. Analyze trends in non-current assets to understand a company's long-term investment strategy.

3. Current Liabilities: Current liabilities are debts that must be paid within one year. Examples include accounts payable, short-term loans, and accrued expenses. Analyze trends in current liabilities to understand a company's short-term liquidity and ability to meet its financial obligations.

4. Long-Term Liabilities: Long-term liabilities are debts that are due beyond one year. Examples include long-term loans and bonds. Analyze trends in long-term liabilities to understand a company's long-term debt management and leverage.

5. Equity: Equity represents the residual value of a company after its liabilities have been subtracted from its assets. Analyze trends in equity to understand a company's financial health and stability.

6. Working Capital: Working capital is calculated as current assets minus current liabilities. A positive working capital indicates a company has enough short-term assets to cover its short-term debts. Analyze trends in working capital to understand a company's liquidity and financial stability.

7. Debt-to-Equity Ratio: The debt-to-equity ratio is calculated as total debt divided by total equity. This ratio provides insights into a company's financial leverage and risk.

Next, move on to the income statement. The income statement

summarizes a company's revenues, expenses, and net income over a period of time. Analyze the income statement to evaluate a company's profitability and earnings potential. Here are the main parameters to look for in an income statement analysis:

1. Revenue: The first line of the income statement is revenue, which represents the total amount of money a company earned during the period. Look for trends in revenue growth over time and compare revenue to industry benchmarks.

2. Gross Profit: Gross profit is the difference between revenue and the cost of goods sold. Analyzing gross profit margins can provide insights into a company's pricing power and cost management.

3. Operating Expenses: Operating expenses include selling, general, and administrative expenses, research and development costs, and other expenses related to running the business. Analyze trends in operating expenses and compare them to industry benchmarks.

4. Operating Income: Operating income is the amount of profit a company earns from its operations before interest and taxes. Analyze trends in operating income and compare them to industry benchmarks.

5. Net Income: Net income is the amount of profit a company earns after all expenses are subtracted. Analyze trends in net income and compare them to industry benchmarks.

6. Earnings Per Share: Earnings per share (EPS) is the amount of net income a company earns per share of its outstanding stock. Analyze trends in EPS and compare them to industry benchmarks.

7. Other Key Metrics: Other key metrics to consider

include return on equity (ROE), return on assets (ROA), and profit margins. Analyze these metrics to gain insights into a company's profitability and efficiency.

Finally, examine the cash flow statement. The cash flow statement tracks the inflow and outflow of cash in a business over a period of time. Analyze the cash flow statement to evaluate a company's liquidity and ability to generate cash. Here are the main parameters to look for in a cash flow statement analysis:

1. Operating Cash Flow: Operating cash flow measures the amount of cash a company generates from its normal business operations. Analyze trends in operating cash flow to understand a company's ability to generate cash from its core business.

2. Investing Cash Flow: Investing cash flow measures the amount of cash a company spends on investments, such as property, plant, and equipment, and the amount of cash it receives from the sale of investments. Analyze trends in investing cash flow to understand a company's investment strategy and growth potential.

3. Financing Cash Flow: Financing cash flow measures the amount of cash a company raises or spends on financing activities, such as issuing or repurchasing stock, paying dividends, and taking on or repaying debt. Analyze trends in financing cash flow to understand a company's financial structure and capital raising activities.

4. Free Cash Flow: Free cash flow measures the amount of cash a company generates after subtracting capital expenditures from operating cash flow. Analyze trends in free cash flow to understand a company's

ability to fund investments, repay debt, and pay dividends.

5. Cash Balance: The ending cash balance on the cash flow statement provides insights into a company's liquidity and cash position.

6. Cash Conversion Cycle: The cash conversion cycle measures the time it takes for a company to convert inventory into cash. Analyze trends in the cash conversion cycle to understand a company's efficiency in managing its working capital.

7. Capital Expenditures: Capital expenditures are investments in long-term assets such as property, plant, and equipment. Analyze trends in capital expenditures to understand a company's investment strategy and potential for future growth.

When analyzing financial statements, it's important to avoid common pitfalls. One common mistake is focusing too much on a single financial metric or ratio. Instead, use multiple ratios to get a comprehensive view of a company's financial health.

Another pitfall to avoid is failing to consider macroeconomic factors. Economic trends and conditions can have a significant impact on a company's financial performance, so it's important to consider these factors when analyzing financial statements.

# CHAPTER 3. IDENTIFYING UNDERVALUED STOCKS USING FUNDAMENTAL ANALYSIS

Identifying undervalued stocks can be a profitable investment strategy for investors who are looking to buy stocks that are trading below their intrinsic value. The principle behind investing in undervalued stocks is to find companies whose stock prices are lower than their true worth, with the expectation that the market will eventually recognize their true value and their stock price will rise.

One of the most fundamental principles for identifying undervalued stocks is to conduct fundamental analysis. Fundamental analysis involves analyzing a company's financial statements, management, industry, and competition to determine its true worth. By analyzing a company's financial statements, investors can determine its profitability, revenue growth, and debt levels. By analyzing its management, industry, and competition, investors can determine its competitive position and its potential for growth.

Another principle for identifying undervalued stocks is to look for stocks that have a low price-to-earnings (P/E) ratio. The P/E ratio is an essential metric because it helps investors understand how much they are paying for each dollar of a company's earnings. A low P/E ratio can indicate that a stock is undervalued, meaning that investors are paying less for each dollar of earnings than they would for a comparable company with a higher P/E ratio. On the other hand, a high P/E ratio can indicate that a stock is overvalued, meaning that investors are paying more for each dollar of earnings than they would for a comparable company with a lower P/E ratio.

Investors can also look for undervalued stocks by examining their price-to-book (P/B) ratio. The P/B ratio compares a company's stock price to its book value per share. The book value per share represents the amount of money that would be returned to shareholders if all of the company's assets were sold and all of its liabilities were paid off. The P/B ratio is an essential metric because it helps investors understand how much they are paying for each dollar of a company's book value. A low P/B ratio can indicate that a stock is undervalued, meaning that investors are paying less for each dollar of book value than they would for a comparable company with a higher P/B ratio. On the other hand, a high P/B ratio can indicate that a stock is overvalued, meaning that investors are paying more for each dollar of book value than they would for a comparable company with a lower P/B ratio.

Another strategy for identifying undervalued stocks is to look for stocks with a high dividend yield. Dividend yield is the ratio of a company's annual dividend payment to its stock price. A high dividend yield can indicate that a company's stock price is lower than its true worth, as investors are receiving a higher return on their investment through dividends.

Value investors also look for stocks that are trading below their historical averages. By examining a company's historical stock price trends, investors can determine whether the company's current stock price is lower than its historical average, which can be a signal that the stock is undervalued.

Investors seek to take advantage of these market inefficiencies by identifying stocks that are undervalued based on their intrinsic value. This intrinsic value is determined by analyzing the company's financial statements, such as its earnings, assets, and liabilities, as well as its industry and competitive position.

Calculating the intrinsic value of a stock involves estimating the present value of the future cash flows that the stock is expected to generate. The basic idea is that the intrinsic value of a stock is equal to the present value of all the cash flows that the stock will generate over its lifetime. Here are the steps to calculate the intrinsic value of a stock:

1. Estimate the future cash flows: The first step is to estimate the future cash flows that the stock is expected to generate. This involves analyzing the company's financial statements, growth prospects, and other relevant factors to estimate the cash flows that the company will generate in the future.

2. Determine the discount rate: The next step is to determine the discount rate, which is the rate at which you will discount the future cash flows to their present value. The discount rate should reflect the risk associated with the investment. For example, if the stock is very risky, you may use a higher discount rate to reflect this risk.

3. Calculate the present value of the cash flows: Once you have estimated the future cash flows and the discount rate, you can calculate the present value of each cash flow by dividing it by (1 + discount rate) raised to the number of years until the cash flow is

expected to be received. Then, add up all the present values of the cash flows to arrive at the total present value of the stock.

4. Compare the intrinsic value to the current stock price: Finally, compare the intrinsic value of the stock to its current market price. If the intrinsic value is higher than the market price, the stock may be undervalued.

# CHAPTER 4. BENJAMIN GRAHAM'S VALUE INVESTING APPROACH

Benjamin Graham was one of the most important figures in the history of investment and finance. Born in London in 1894, Graham immigrated to the United States with his family at a young age. His early years were marked by financial hardship, but his intellect and work ethic would eventually lead him to become a highly successful investor, author, and professor.

His first experience with investing came as a young man, when he inherited a small sum of money from his grandfather. Initially, he was hesitant to invest the money, but eventually decided to put it into the stock market. This decision proved fortuitous, as Graham quickly realized that he had a natural talent for investing. He spent the next several years honing his skills, studying financial statements and analyzing market trends.

After completing his undergraduate degree at Columbia University, Graham went on to study at the university's business school. There, he was mentored by legendary investor David Dodd, with whom he would later co-author the seminal investment book "Security Analysis." Graham also worked for a time as a securities analyst for the Newburger, Henderson & Loeb brokerage firm, where he gained practical experience in the investment industry.

In the 1930s, Graham began teaching investment courses at Columbia. His approach to investing was based on the concept of "value investing", which emphasized the importance of buying stocks at a discount to their intrinsic value. Graham believed that careful analysis of financial statements could reveal companies that were undervalued by the market, and that investing in these companies could generate superior returns over the long term.

His investment philosophy proved prescient, as he was able to generate significant returns for his clients during the Great Depression. He famously recommended that investors buy stocks when they were "on the bargain counter", and he practiced what he preached by investing heavily in companies that were trading at significant discounts to their book value.

Over the years, Graham's reputation as an investment guru grew, and he became a sought-after speaker and consultant. He continued to teach at Columbia until his retirement in 1957, and his ideas and teachings have influenced generations of investors.

One of the most significant contributions that Graham made to the field of investing was his emphasis on the importance of intrinsic value. Graham believed that a stock's value was determined by its intrinsic value, which was based on the company's financial position, earnings, and other fundamental factors. He believed that a stock was only worth buying if it was trading at a significant discount to its intrinsic value, as this provided a margin of safety for investors.

Graham also popularized the concept of "Mr. Market," which he used to describe the irrational behavior of the stock market. Graham believed that the stock market was often driven by emotions, such as fear and greed, and that this could lead to stocks being mispriced. He encouraged investors to take advantage of these mispricing's by buying stocks that were undervalued by the market.

One example of Graham's value investing strategy in action was his investment in the Northern Pipeline Company in the early 1930s. At the time, Northern Pipeline was trading at a significant discount to its intrinsic value, as the market had not yet recognized the value of the company's assets. Graham recognized the opportunity to buy the company's stock at a discount and held it for several years until the market caught up, earning substantial returns on his investment.

Another significant contribution that Graham made to the field of investing was his emphasis on risk management. Graham believed that investors should focus on minimizing their downside risk, rather than maximizing their upside potential. Here are some of the key indicators that Benjamin Graham used to analyze a stock:

1. Price-to-earnings (P/E) ratio: He believed that the P/E ratio was one of the most important metrics for evaluating a stock. The P/E ratio compares the current market price of a stock to its earnings per share. Graham preferred stocks with a P/E ratio of less than 15.

2. Price-to-book (P/B) ratio: The P/B ratio compares the current market price of a stock to its book value per share. Graham preferred stocks with a P/B ratio of less than 1.5.

3. Dividend yield: He believed that stocks that paid a consistent dividend were often undervalued by the market. He preferred stocks with a dividend yield of at least 4%.

4. Earnings per share (EPS) growth rate: Graham believed that a company's earnings growth rate was a key indicator of its future success. He preferred companies with a consistent EPS growth rate of at least 7% per year.

5. Debt-to-equity ratio: He believed that a company's debt level was an important factor to consider when analyzing a stock. He preferred companies with a debt-to-equity ratio of less than 1.

It's important to note that Graham did not rely solely on these indicators when analyzing stocks. He believed in conducting a thorough analysis of a company's financial statements, management team, industry trends, and other factors before making an investment decision.

One of his most famous investments was in the Government Employees Insurance Company, or GEICO, an insurance company that he purchased in the 1940s. At the time, GEICO was a small, regional insurance company that was struggling financially. However, Graham saw potential in the company and began to purchase its stock. He believed that the company was undervalued by the market, and that its strong management team and low overhead costs would allow it to thrive in the long term.

His investment in GEICO was significant, with his investment firm, Graham-Newman Corp., eventually holding a 50% stake in the company. He and his partner, Jerome Newman, purchased the first shares of GEICO for $27 per share in 1948, when the company was trading at a discount to its book value.

Over the next few years, Graham continued to purchase shares in GEICO as the company's financial performance improved. His investment in the company was so successful that he referred to it as his "best investment". By the time he sold his stake in the company in the 1970s, the value of his investment had grown significantly.

In total, Graham's investment in GEICO earned him and his clients returns of over 20 times their initial investment. In 1972, when he sold his shares, the company was trading at a price of $348 per share, which was more than ten times the price at which he had originally purchased the stock.

His success with GEICO can be attributed to his adherence to value investing principles. He recognized that the company was undervalued by the market and had strong fundamentals that would allow it to grow in the long term. He also had the patience and discipline to hold onto his investment through ups and downs, allowing it to grow in value over time.

Graham's impact on value investing has been significant and long-lasting. His principles and ideas continue to be studied and practiced by investors around the world. In addition, Graham's emphasis on risk management and his focus on intrinsic value have become essential components of modern portfolio management.

# CHAPTER 5. JOHN NEFF'S VALUE INVESTING APPROACH

John Neff is a well-known investment manager and former managing partner at Wellington Management Company. He is widely recognized for his exceptional performance as the manager of the Vanguard Windsor Fund, which he managed from 1964 to 1995. Neff's early days were marked by hard work, persistence, and an unrelenting desire to succeed.

He was born on June 19, 1931, in Wauseon, Ohio, to parents who were farmers. He was the youngest of three children and grew up in a small, rural community. Neff's parents instilled in him the value of hard work and the importance of education. He excelled in school, particularly in mathematics, and was awarded a scholarship to attend the University of Toledo.

Neff graduated from the University of Toledo in 1955 with a degree in business administration. After graduation, he began his career as an investment analyst at the National City Bank of Cleveland. He quickly made a name for himself as a talented analyst and was promoted to the position of portfolio manager in 1960.

In 1964, Neff joined Wellington Management Company in Philadelphia, where he became the manager of the Vanguard Windsor Fund. At the time, the fund was struggling and had underperformed the market for several years. Neff recognized the potential of the fund and set about implementing a value investing strategy that focused on buying undervalued stocks.

His strategy proved to be extremely successful, and he was able to generate exceptional returns for the fund's investors. Over the next 31 years, Neff grew the Vanguard Windsor Fund from $18 million to $13 billion, and the fund outperformed the S&P 500 by an average of 3.1% per year. Neff's success was attributed to his ability to identify undervalued stocks and to patiently wait for them to appreciate in value.

In the early 1980s, Ford was facing significant challenges. At the time, Ford was trading at a low P/E ratio of around 5, which Neff believed was undervalued given the company's strong fundamentals. The American auto industry was struggling with high inflation, rising fuel prices, and intense foreign competition, particularly from Japanese automakers. In addition, Ford was burdened with high labor costs, outdated factories, and a reputation for producing low-quality vehicles. The company's stock price reflected these challenges, and it was trading at a deep discount to its book value.

Neff saw an opportunity in Ford's undervalued stock price and decided to invest in the company. He believed that Ford's management was taking steps to turn the company around, such as cutting costs, improving quality, and introducing new models. He also saw potential in Ford's international operations, particularly in Europe and Asia.

Neff's investment in Ford was significant. At one point, the Windsor Fund held as much as 7% of Ford's outstanding shares, making it one of the largest institutional shareholders in the company. Neff continued to hold onto Ford's stock for several years, even as the stock price fluctuated. By the time he retired in 1995, Ford had become one of the top performers in the Windsor Fund.

Neff's investment philosophy was centered around the idea of buying stocks that were trading at a discount to their intrinsic value. He believed that the market was often inefficient and that by doing thorough research, he could identify stocks that were undervalued. Neff was also a long-term investor and was willing to hold onto stocks for several years, even if they did not immediately appreciate in value. Here are some key indicators that John Neff used to analyze stocks:

1. Price-to-earnings ratio (P/E ratio): Neff believed that a stock's P/E ratio was a crucial indicator of its value. He looked for stocks with a lower P/E ratio than their industry peers, as this indicated that the stock was undervalued and had room to grow.

2. Price-to-book ratio (P/B ratio): This ratio measures a company's market value in relation to its book value. Neff preferred stocks with a lower P/B ratio, as this suggested that the stock was undervalued relative to its assets.

3. Dividend yield: He also looked for stocks with a high dividend yield, as this indicated that the company was financially stable and had the potential to provide a steady income stream to investors.

4. Earnings growth: Neff analyzed a company's earnings growth rate over time to assess its potential for future growth. He looked for companies with a consistent track record of strong earnings growth.

5. Return on equity (ROE): This measures a company's profitability relative to its shareholders' equity. Neff looked for companies with a high ROE, as this indicated that the company was efficient in generating profits from its equity.

One controversial aspect of Neff's investment strategy was his investment in tobacco companies. Neff began buying shares of tobacco companies in the 1980s, including Philip Morris, RJ Reynolds, and Brown & Williamson. At the time, tobacco companies were facing increasing regulatory pressure and public scrutiny due to the health risks associated with smoking. However, Neff saw an opportunity to invest in these companies while they were undervalued by the market.

Neff's investment in tobacco companies paid off handsomely over the years. By the time he retired in 1995, tobacco stocks had become some of the top performers in the Windsor Fund. Philip Morris, for example, had grown from $0.56 per share in 1977 to $35 per share in 1995. Brown & Williamson had similarly impressive growth, with its stock price rising from $4.25 in 1980 to $36.50 in 1995.

Despite the controversy surrounding his investment in tobacco companies, Neff defended his decision by pointing out that tobacco stocks were undervalued by the market and offered high dividend yields. He also argued that tobacco companies were not going to go out of business anytime soon, and that the risks associated with smoking were well-known to the public.

# CHAPTER 6. SETH KLARMAN'S VALUE INVESTING APPROACH

Seth Klarman was born in 1957 in New York City. He grew up in a Jewish family in Baltimore, Maryland, and attended Cornell University, where he earned a degree in economics. After graduating from Cornell, Klarman went on to attend Harvard Business School, where he earned an MBA in 1982.

After finishing business school, Klarman took a job with the mutual fund group, Max Heine & Stedman, where he worked as an analyst. During his time at Max Heine & Stedman, Klarman began to develop his investment philosophy, which emphasized value investing and the importance of risk management.

In 1982, Klarman left Max Heine & Stedman to start his own investment firm, the Baupost Group. The Baupost Group was initially funded with just $27 million in assets, but Klarman quickly began to build a reputation as a successful investor. Klarman's approach to investing was different from the prevailing wisdom of the time, which emphasized growth and momentum investing. Instead, Klarman focused on finding undervalued assets that had been overlooked by the market.

One example of his value investing strategy in action was his investment in the real estate investment trust (REIT) industry in the 1990s. Klarman recognized that the REIT industry was undervalued by the market due to concerns about rising interest rates and oversupply of real estate. However, Klarman believed that these concerns were overblown and that the REIT industry was a strong business with predictable cash flows. Klarman purchased REIT stocks for The Baupost Group and held them for several years, eventually selling them for substantial profits as the market recognized the value of the industry.

While Klarman is known for being somewhat secretive about his investment strategy, he has discussed his approach to analyzing stocks in various writings and interviews. Here are some key indicators that Seth Klarman use to analyze a stock:

1. Margin of Safety: Klarman is known for emphasizing the importance of a margin of safety when investing. Essentially, this means that he looks for stocks that are undervalued by the market, providing a cushion against potential losses.

2. Free Cash Flow: He pays close attention to a company's free cash flow, which is the cash generated by a business after accounting for capital expenditures. Free cash flow is a critical measure of a company's financial health and can give insight into whether a company is reinvesting profits wisely or has room for growth.

3. Book Value: He also looks at a company's book value, which is the value of a company's assets minus its liabilities. This gives an indication of what the company would be worth if it were to be liquidated.

4. Competitive Advantage: Klarman looks for companies with a sustainable competitive advantage, such as a unique product or service, a strong brand, or a large market share. A company with a competitive advantage is more likely to generate stable and predictable earnings.

During the 2008 financial crisis, his investment philosophy was put to the test. As a value investor, Klarman was always on the lookout for investment opportunities that were undervalued by the market. The financial crisis provided Klarman with a unique opportunity to put his investment philosophy into practice by investing in distressed debt securities of bankrupt companies.

He saw an opportunity to buy debt securities of companies that were in bankruptcy proceedings at a deep discount to their face value. These distressed debt securities were often trading at pennies on the dollar, which presented a significant upside potential if the companies were able to emerge from bankruptcy and recover.

Klarman was not deterred by the high degree of risk associated with investing in distressed debt securities. He recognized that there was a significant amount of uncertainty associated with investing in bankrupt companies, but he believed that the potential rewards outweighed the risks.

His investment in the distressed debt of bankrupt companies was a bold move, but it paid off handsomely for his fund. Klarman purchased these distressed debt securities for his fund and held them until the companies emerged from bankruptcy, earning substantial returns as the securities increased in value.

In 2018, Seth Klarman's Baupost Group disclosed a significant investment in Micron Technology, a leading producer of dynamic random-access memory (DRAM) and NAND flash memory chips. Klarman's investment in Micron was significant, with the Baupost Group purchasing over 11 million shares of the company at an average cost of around $47 per share.

So, what was the investment rationale behind Klarman's decision to invest in Micron?

First, Klarman likely recognized that Micron was a market leader in the DRAM and NAND flash memory chip industries. These are key components of many electronic devices, and the demand for these chips has been growing rapidly in recent years. With Micron's strong position in these markets, Klarman likely saw an opportunity for significant growth in the coming years.

Second, Klarman may have been attracted to Micron's relatively low valuation compared to its peers. Micron had a price-to-earnings ratio (P/E) of around 6 at the time of Klarman's investment, while many other companies in the technology industry had significantly higher P/Es. This may have indicated that Micron was undervalued by the market, presenting an opportunity for Klarman to generate significant returns if the market eventually recognized the company's true value.

Third, Klarman likely recognized the significant barriers to entry in the DRAM and NAND flash memory chip industries. These barriers include high capital requirements, complex manufacturing processes, and intellectual property protection. With Micron's strong position in these industries, Klarman may have seen a competitive advantage that would be difficult for other companies to overcome.

Finally, Klarman may have been attracted to Micron's strong balance sheet and cash flow generation. Micron had significant cash reserves and generated strong free cash flow, indicating that the company was financially stable and had the ability to invest in future growth opportunities. In the end, his investment in Micron proved to be successful, with the company's stock price increasing significantly in the years following Klarman's investment.

# CHAPTER 7. PHILIP FISHER'S GROWTH INVESTING APPROACH

Philip Fisher, born on September 8, 1907, was an American stock investor and author, best known for his philosophy of long-term investing in growth stocks. He spent his early days in the San Francisco Bay Area, California, where he was raised by his parents, who were both in the printing business.

He was an intelligent student, and he graduated from Stanford University in 1928 with a degree in economics. After completing his education, he began his career in investment banking with the Anglo-California Trust Company, where he worked as a securities analyst. In 1931, Fisher joined the firm of Kieckhefer Corporation, where he worked as a securities analyst until 1939.

During his tenure at Kieckhefer Corporation, Fisher developed his investment philosophy, which was based on extensive research and analysis of the companies he was considering investing in. He believed that long-term investments in high-quality companies with strong management teams and competitive advantages were the key to achieving success in the stock market.

In 1939, Fisher started his own investment advisory firm, Fisher & Company, which became known for its research-driven investment strategies. Fisher's approach to investing was unique for its time, as he emphasized the importance of conducting in-depth research and analysis of a company's financial statements, as well as interviewing management teams and suppliers to gain a better understanding of a company's competitive advantages.

In the early 1950s, Fisher gained recognition as an expert in the field of growth investing, which focuses on finding companies that are expected to grow at a higher rate than the overall market. His book, "Common Stocks and Uncommon Profits," which was first published in 1958, became a classic in the field of investing and is still widely read by investors today.

One of Fisher's most successful investments was in Motorola, a telecommunications company that was at the forefront of the emerging mobile phone industry in the 1980s. Fisher recognized early on that mobile phones had the potential to become a ubiquitous technology, and he saw Motorola as one of the key players in the industry.

Fisher began investing in Motorola in the late 1970s, when the company's stock price was relatively low. Over the next several years, he continued to add to his position in the company as Motorola's mobile phone business began to take off.

By the mid-1980s, Fisher's investment in Motorola had paid off handsomely. The company's mobile phone business was growing rapidly, and its stock price had risen dramatically. Fisher had bought shares of Motorola for around $3 per share, and by the time he sold his position, the stock price had risen to over $80 per share. Overall, Fisher's investment in Motorola had earned him a massive profit.

Another of Fisher's successful investments was in Texas Instruments, a technology company that was at the forefront of the emerging semiconductor industry in the 1960s. Fisher recognized early on that semiconductors had the potential to revolutionize the electronics industry, and he saw Texas Instruments as one of the key players in the industry.

Fisher began investing in Texas Instruments in the early 1960s, when the company's stock price was relatively low. Over the next several years, he continued to add to his position in the company as Texas Instruments' semiconductor business began to take off.

By the late 1960s, Fisher's investment in Texas Instruments had paid off handsomely. The company's semiconductor business was growing rapidly, and its stock price had risen dramatically. Fisher had bought shares of Texas Instruments for around $10 per share, and by the time he sold his position, the stock price had risen to over $200 per share.

Philip Fisher's success as a growth investor was built on his ability to identify companies with strong growth potential and a focus on long-term value creation. His investments in companies like Motorola and Texas Instruments demonstrate the power of growth investing, and his legacy continues to inspire investors today.

Warren Buffett, widely regarded as one of the greatest investors of all time, was greatly influenced by Philip Fisher's investment philosophy. Fisher's emphasis on thorough research and long-term investment in high-quality companies was a major influence on Buffett's investment style.

Buffett admired Fisher's approach to investing, and the two became friends and often corresponded about investing strategies. Buffett has credited Fisher with helping him develop his own investment philosophy. Buffett has said that Fisher's book "Common Stocks and Uncommon Profits" was one of the most important investment books he ever read. He has applied Fisher's principles in his own investing career, focusing on long-term investment in high-quality companies with strong competitive advantages. Buffett has often talked about his focus on a company's "economic moat," or its ability to maintain its competitive advantage over time. He has also emphasized the importance of understanding a company's management, a principle he learned from Fisher. Buffett has said that he looks for companies with honest, competent, and shareholder-friendly management.

# PART 3. TECHNICAL ANALYSIS

*"Technical analysis is not a perfect crystal ball. It is a tool that can help you gain insight into the market, but it is not a substitute for good judgment, solid research, and disciplined trading habits."*

*Jack D. Schwager*

# CHAPTER 8. UNDERSTANDING CHARTS AND INDICATORS

Understanding charts and indicators is a crucial part of predicting market trends. Charts can provide visual representations of a stock's price movement over time, while indicators can offer insights into a stock's momentum and potential direction. Here are some key steps to understanding charts and indicators:

1. Learn the basics of technical analysis: Technical analysis is the practice of using charts and indicators to predict future price movements in the stock market. To get started, it's important to understand some of the key concepts and terminology associated with technical analysis.

2. Study different chart types: There are several different types of charts used in technical analysis, including line charts, bar charts, and candlestick charts. Each chart type has its own strengths and weaknesses, and it's important to understand how to interpret them correctly.

3. Identify key support and resistance levels: Support and resistance levels are areas where the price of a

stock has historically shown to stop and reverse its trend. Identifying these levels can provide insight into potential buying and selling opportunities.

4. Use technical indicators to confirm trends: Technical indicators are calculations based on the price and/ or volume of a stock. These indicators can provide valuable insights into a stock's momentum and potential direction. Some common indicators include moving averages, Relative Strength Index (RSI), and Moving Average Convergence Divergence (MACD).

5. Stay up-to-date with market news and events: While technical analysis can be a powerful tool for predicting market trends, it's important to also stay informed about broader economic and industry trends. News events such as changes in interest rates, geopolitical tensions, or industry disruptions can have a significant impact on the stock market.

By studying different chart types, identifying support and resistance levels, using technical indicators to confirm trends, and staying up-to-date with market news and events, investors can gain valuable insights into potential buying and selling opportunities in the stock market. While technical analysis is not foolproof and should be combined with fundamental analysis, it can be a powerful tool for making informed investment decisions.

Paul Tudor Jones is a legendary investor and hedge fund manager who founded Tudor Investment Corporation in 1980. In the fall of 1987, Jones was monitoring the stock market closely, as he sensed that a major correction was looming. His analysis of the market was based on both fundamental and technical factors, but it was his understanding of charts that ultimately led him to make a bold and lucrative trade.

On October 19, 1987, the stock market experienced a sudden

and severe drop, with the Dow Jones Industrial Average falling more than 22% in a single day. Many investors panicked and sold off their holdings, but Jones saw an opportunity. He had been tracking the movement of the S&P 500 index on a daily chart and noticed a key level of support at 215. If the index fell below that level, he believed it could trigger a wave of selling and push the market even lower.

Jones made a bold move and placed a massive bet against the market, buying put options on the S&P 500 index. His analysis proved to be correct, as the market continued to decline over the next few days. By the end of October, the market had lost more than a third of its value, but Jones' trade had earned him a profit of over $100 million.

His success in the 1987 crash was not just a stroke of luck or a random gamble. It was the result of his disciplined approach to analyzing the market and his deep understanding of technical analysis. By carefully studying charts and identifying key levels of support and resistance, Jones was able to make a well-informed and profitable trade in a time of extreme market volatility.

# CHAPTER 9. IDENTIFYING HIGH-GROWTH COMPANIES USING TECHNICAL ANALYSIS

Identifying high-growth companies can be a profitable investment strategy for investors who are willing to take on more risk in pursuit of higher returns. High-growth companies are those that are experiencing significant revenue and earnings growth and have the potential to continue to grow at a rapid pace in the future.

One principle for identifying high-growth companies is to look for companies that are operating in industries with strong growth prospects. For example, companies in industries such as technology, healthcare, and renewable energy may have strong growth prospects due to trends such as increased adoption of technology, an aging population, and a shift towards clean energy.

These parameters can help investors determine a company's potential for future growth and assess the company's overall financial health:

    1. Revenue Growth: One of the most important

parameters to look for in a high-growth company is revenue growth. High-growth companies typically have a history of strong revenue growth and are expected to continue to grow at a rapid pace in the future.

2. Earnings Growth: Earnings growth is another important parameter to consider. Companies that are able to increase their earnings at a rapid pace may have a higher potential for future growth.

3. Profit Margins: Profit margins are a measure of a company's profitability. Companies with higher profit margins may be able to reinvest more money into the business and fuel future growth.

4. Return on Equity (ROE): ROE is a measure of how effectively a company is using shareholder equity to generate profits. Companies with a high ROE may have a higher potential for future growth.

5. Total Addressable Market (TAM): The TAM represents the total market opportunity for a company's products or services. Companies with a large TAM may have a higher potential for future growth as they capture a larger share of the market.

6. Competitive Advantage: Companies with a competitive advantage, such as a unique product or service, may be better positioned to grow at a rapid pace.

7. Management: The quality of a company's management team can also be an important factor in assessing a company's potential for growth. Strong management teams may be better equipped to navigate challenges and capitalize on growth opportunities.

The stock market is known for its volatility, which refers to the rapid and unpredictable changes in the value of stocks and other securities. Market volatility can have a significant impact on investors, affecting their portfolio returns and investment decisions. Understanding stock market volatility and how to navigate it can be essential for investors looking to achieve their financial goals.

Market volatility can be caused by a variety of factors, including changes in economic conditions, political events, company news, and global events. When investors perceive a higher level of risk, they may sell off their investments, leading to a decline in stock prices. Similarly, when investors perceive a lower level of risk, they may buy more investments, leading to an increase in stock prices.

In the early 2000s, investor Mark Minervini used technical analysis to identify high-growth stocks and achieved a remarkable return of 33,554% over a five-year period. One of the stocks he invested in was Priceline.com, an online travel booking company.

Minervini noticed that Priceline's stock had been showing strong momentum on its chart, with a series of higher highs and higher lows. He also noticed that the company's earnings and sales growth were accelerating rapidly, indicating that it was poised for significant future growth.

Based on his analysis, Minervini made a bold move and purchased a large position in Priceline, using a combination of both technical and fundamental analysis. His investment paid off handsomely, as Priceline's stock price soared from around $10 per share in 2003 to over $1,000 per share by 2018.

His success in identifying high-growth companies using technical analysis was the result of his disciplined approach to analyzing stocks and his deep understanding of technical indicators. By carefully studying charts and identifying key trends and patterns, he was able to spot companies with strong potential for growth and profit from their success.

While market volatility can be unsettling, it's important to remember that it's a natural part of investing in the stock market. Historically, the stock market has shown a tendency to trend upwards over the long term, despite short-term fluctuations. However, navigating market volatility can still be challenging for investors.

# CHAPTER 10. WILLIAM O'NEIL'S MOMENTUM INVESTING APPROACH

William O'Neil was born on March 25, 1933, in Oklahoma City, Oklahoma. His family moved to California when he was a child, and he grew up in Pasadena. As a teenager, O'Neil was interested in business and investing. He began investing in stocks at the age of 21 with just $500 he had saved from working odd jobs.

In 1958, O'Neil founded his first company, the O'Neil Data Systems. The company specialized in providing research data for stockbrokers and institutional investors. O'Neil's unique approach to data analysis and stock market research quickly gained the attention of the financial industry. He started the investment newsletter, Investor's Business Daily (IBD) in 1963. The publication's main focus was on providing investors with data and analysis to help them make informed investment decisions. IBD quickly became one of the most popular investment newsletters in the country.

During the 1970s, O'Neil's reputation as an investment expert continued to grow. He became a regular guest on television and radio shows, offering his insights on the stock market and investing.

His investment philosophy revolves around the concept of buying stocks that show strong momentum in their price and earnings growth. He uses a combination of technical and fundamental analysis to identify stocks that have strong momentum, and he places a strong emphasis on cutting losses quickly if a stock's momentum begins to weaken. Here is a step-by-step guide explaining how William O'Neil invests in stocks:

1. Look for Companies with Strong Fundamentals: His approach to investing starts with identifying companies with strong fundamentals, such as high earnings growth, high return on equity (ROE), and low debt-to-equity ratios. He believes that companies with strong fundamentals are more likely to outperform the market over the long term.

2. Identify Industry Groups with Strong Momentum: After identifying companies with strong fundamentals, O'Neil looks for industry groups that are showing strong momentum. He believes that investing in industry groups that are in an uptrend is more likely to result in higher returns. He uses IBD's proprietary industry group rankings to identify industry groups with strong momentum.

3. Look for Stocks with Strong Technicals: Once O'Neil has identified industry groups with strong momentum, he looks for individual stocks within those groups that are showing strong technicals. He uses a combination of chart patterns, such as cup-and-handle, double bottom, and flat base, to identify stocks that are poised to make a big move.

4. Check the Market Direction: Before making any trades, he checks the overall market direction to ensure that the market is in an uptrend. He uses IBD's proprietary market trend indicators to assess the overall health of the market.

5. Buy Stocks with Strong Technicals and

Fundamentals: Once O'Neil has identified stocks with strong technicals and fundamentals, he waits for a proper buy point to enter the trade. He uses a combination of chart patterns and technical indicators, such as moving averages and relative strength, to identify the optimal time to buy.

6. Monitor Stocks Closely: After entering a trade, he closely monitors the stock's performance and adjusts his position accordingly. He uses a combination of stop-loss orders and profit targets to manage risk and maximize returns.

7. Sell Stocks that are Underperforming: If a stock is not performing as expected, O'Neil will sell the position and move on to other opportunities. He believes in cutting losses quickly and moving on to the next trade.

In the early 1980s, Walmart was a relatively unknown discount retailer that was trading at a low valuation. However, William O'Neil saw the potential for the company to grow and become a dominant player in the retail industry. He believed that Walmart's low-cost business model and focus on customer service would enable it to outperform its competitors over the long term.

O'Neil's investment in Walmart was based on a combination of fundamental and technical analysis. He recognized that Walmart had strong fundamentals, such as high earnings growth, high return on equity (ROE), and low debt-to-equity ratios. He also saw that the company was expanding rapidly, with plans to open new stores across the country. This combination of strong fundamentals and growth potential made Walmart an attractive investment opportunity.

In addition to fundamental analysis, O'Neil also used technical analysis to identify the optimal time to buy Walmart's stock.

He saw that the stock was trading in a tight range and was showing signs of accumulation by institutional investors. This was a bullish sign that suggested that the stock was poised for a breakout.

His investment in Walmart was not without risk. At the time, the retail industry was highly competitive, with many established players vying for market share. However, O'Neil believed that Walmart's low-cost business model and focus on customer service would enable it to outperform its competitors over the long term.

Over the next decade, O'Neil's investment in Walmart proved to be a wise decision. The company grew rapidly, opening new stores across the country and expanding into new markets. Walmart became a dominant player in the retail industry, with a market capitalization of over $100 billion by the late 1990s.

When analyzing stocks, he relied on several key indicators to identify stocks with strong momentum and growth potential. Here are some of the key indicators that O'Neil used to analyze stocks:

1. Earnings Per Share (EPS): One of the most important fundamental indicators for O'Neil was a company's earnings per share. He looked for companies with strong EPS growth rates over the past few quarters and years. Companies with strong EPS growth rates are often expected to continue to grow in the future and have strong momentum.

2. Sales Growth: O'Neil also looked at a company's sales growth rate, as this can be a good indicator of a company's potential for future earnings growth. He looked for companies with strong sales growth rates over the past few quarters and years.

3. Relative Price Strength: Another key technical

indicator that O'Neil used was relative price strength. This measures how well a stock has performed compared to other stocks in the same industry or sector. O'Neil looked for stocks that were outperforming their peers in terms of price strength.

4. Volume: He also paid close attention to trading volume, as this can indicate whether there is strong interest in a stock. He looked for stocks that had strong trading volume, as this can be a sign of momentum.

5. Chart Patterns: He used technical analysis to look for chart patterns that indicate a stock is likely to continue its upward trend. He looked for stocks with cup-and-handle patterns or stocks that had formed a strong base before breaking out.

Another example of O'Neil's success with momentum investing is his investment in Baidu Inc., a Chinese search engine company. In 2006, O'Neil purchased shares of Baidu at a price of around $100 per share. Baidu had recently gone public, and O'Neil saw the potential for the company to grow in the rapidly expanding Chinese market. As Baidu's earnings and stock price continued to grow, O'Neil held onto his shares, eventually selling them in 2011 for a profit of over $900 per share.

His successful application of momentum investing principles has resulted in significant profits over the years. However, it's important to note that not all of his investments have been successful, and O'Neil has also experienced losses at times. Nonetheless, his ability to identify stocks with strong momentum and his willingness to cut losses quickly when necessary has helped him to achieve success in the market.

# CHAPTER 11.
# RICHARD DRIEHAUS' MOMENTUM INVESTING APPROACH

Richard Driehaus is a well-known investor and philanthropist who has made a significant impact in the world of finance over the course of his career. Born in 1942, Driehaus grew up in a middle-class family in Chicago and developed an early interest in business and finance.

After completing his undergraduate studies at DePaul University, Driehaus began his career in finance as a stockbroker, working for a number of different firms in Chicago. During this time, he developed an interest in investing and began to experiment with different investment strategies.

In the 1970s, Driehaus founded his own investment firm, Driehaus Capital Management, with the goal of developing an investment approach that focused on identifying emerging trends and investing in companies that were well-positioned to benefit from those trends. This approach, which would later be known as momentum investing, would become the cornerstone of Driehaus's investment philosophy over the years.

In the early days of his career, Driehaus faced a number of challenges as he worked to establish his firm and develop his investment approach. He struggled to attract clients at first, and he often had to rely on personal connections and word-of-mouth referrals to build his business.

Despite these challenges, Driehaus remained committed to his vision, and he continued to refine his investment approach over time. He began to focus on identifying companies that were experiencing strong positive momentum in the market, and he developed a number of tools and techniques to help him identify these trends:

1. Relative Strength: One of the key tools that Richard Driehaus used to identify stock trends was relative strength. Relative strength is a measure of how well a stock is performing relative to the broader market. Driehaus believed that stocks with high relative strength were more likely to continue to perform well in the future. He used a number of technical indicators, such as moving averages and momentum oscillators, to identify stocks with high relative strength.

2. Earnings Growth: He also believed that earnings growth was an important factor in identifying stocks with strong momentum. He looked for companies that were experiencing strong earnings growth and had the potential to continue to grow earnings in the future. Driehaus would often invest in companies that were experiencing earnings surprises, or that had recently announced positive earnings guidance.

3. Chart Patterns: Driehaus was a firm believer in technical analysis, and he used a number of chart patterns to help him identify stock trends. He looked for stocks that were breaking out of consolidation patterns, such as triangles and rectangles, and he also looked for stocks that were forming bullish

continuation patterns, such as flags and pennants.

4. Sector Analysis: He recognized that stock trends often occur within sectors or industries, and he used sector analysis to identify these trends. He would often focus on sectors that were experiencing strong earnings growth or that were benefiting from broader macroeconomic trends.

5. Stop Losses: Driehaus used stop losses to manage risk in his portfolio. He would set stop losses at predetermined levels, and he would sell a stock if it fell below these levels. This helped him to limit losses and preserve capital in his portfolio.

Driehaus has been successful in using this strategy over the years, and his investment philosophy has helped him generate significant returns on his investments. In the mid-1990s, Driehaus invested in Dell, which was then a relatively unknown company. He paid around $1.50 per share and purchased a significant stake in the company. Driehaus believed that Dell's direct-to-consumer model, focus on customization, and efficient supply chain management made it a strong player in the growing computer industry. He also noted the company's strong earnings growth and positive earnings surprises as reasons to invest.

Over the next several years, Dell's stock price soared as the company's revenues and earnings continued to grow. Driehaus took advantage of the strong momentum in the stock and sold his position for a substantial profit. He reportedly earned more than ten times his initial investment, with the stock reaching a peak of over $50 per share.

He also made a successful investment in Intel, a leading manufacturer of computer processors, in the early 2000s. He paid around $16 per share and made a significant investment in the company. Driehaus recognized that the technology sector was undergoing significant changes at the time, with the growth of the internet and the increasing demand for high-speed processing power. He believed that Intel was well-positioned to benefit from these trends due to its strong research and development capabilities and dominant market position.

Additionally, Driehaus noted that Intel's earnings growth had been consistently strong, with positive earnings surprises in multiple quarters. He also recognized the company's strong balance sheet and dividend history as reasons to invest.

Over the next several years, Intel's stock price continued to climb as the company's earnings growth remained strong. Driehaus was able to take advantage of this momentum, selling his position for a significant profit. He reportedly earned more than three times his initial investment, with the stock reaching a peak of over $70 per share.

However, Driehaus also faced some setbacks as a result of his momentum investing strategy. For example, during the dot-com bubble in the early 2000s, many of the technology stocks that he had invested in experienced significant losses as the market corrected. As a result, Driehaus lost a significant portion of his net worth during this time.

Despite these setbacks, Driehaus continued to believe in the potential of momentum investing, and he remained committed to the strategy over the long term. He continued to invest in stocks that exhibited strong positive momentum, such as Google and Amazon, and he was able to generate significant returns from these investments over time.

In the mid-2010s, he made a successful investment in Netflix, the streaming video company, based on his assessment of the company's long-term growth potential. Driehaus recognized that the traditional TV model was undergoing significant changes with the growth of streaming services. He saw Netflix as a leading player in this space, with a growing subscriber base and a focus on producing original content. He believed that the company's strong brand, growing library of original programming, and global expansion plans made it a strong investment opportunity.

He also noted that Netflix's earnings growth had been consistently strong, with positive earnings surprises in multiple quarters. He recognized the company's strong financials, with a solid balance sheet and a healthy cash flow. Additionally, Driehaus noted that Netflix was benefiting from the trend towards cord-cutting, as more and more consumers were switching to streaming services.

Driehaus made his initial investment in Netflix in 2014 when the stock was trading around $60 per share. Over the next several years, Netflix's stock price soared as the company's revenues and earnings continued to grow. Driehaus took advantage of the strong momentum in the stock and continued to increase his position. He reportedly earned more than five times his initial investment, with the stock reaching a peak of over $400 per share.

After making a considerable profit, Driehaus decided to sell his position in Netflix. He observed that the stock's valuation had become stretched and the company was facing increasing competition from other streaming services in a crowded market. While he had experienced success with the investment, Driehaus believed that it was crucial to recognize when to take profits and move on to other opportunities.

# PART 4. QUANTITATIVE ANALYSIS

*"Certainly, understanding the fundamentals of a company is critical for making informed investment decisions. However, it's important to remember that the markets are driven by human behavior, and human behavior can be unpredictable. Quantitative analysis provides a systematic approach to analyzing market data and identifying patterns that may not be immediately visible to the naked eye. By using data to inform our investment decisions, we can reduce the influence of emotions and biases and make more objective, informed decisions. In today's data-rich world, investors who fail to embrace quantitative analysis are at a significant disadvantage."*

*James P. O'Shaughnessy*

# CHAPTER 12. RIDING THE TRENDS TO MAXIMIZE YOUR RETURNS

Riding the trends is a popular investment strategy that involves identifying stocks that are showing strong momentum and holding onto them for an extended period of time. This approach is based on the idea that stocks that have been trending in one direction are likely to continue trending in that direction for a period of time.

To effectively ride the trends, investors must first identify stocks that are showing strong momentum. This can be done using technical analysis, which involves analyzing a stock's price and volume charts to identify patterns and trends.

Once a strong trend has been identified, the investor can then take a position in the stock and hold onto it for an extended period of time. This approach is known as trend following, and it can be an effective way to maximize returns in the stock market.

One of the key advantages of riding the trends is that it allows investors to capture the full potential of a stock's upward momentum. By holding onto the stock for an extended period of time, investors can benefit from continued price appreciation and potentially earn higher returns than they would by trading in and out of the stock.

However, it's important to note that riding the trends also comes with some risks. Stocks can experience sudden and unexpected downturns, and holding onto a stock for too long can result in significant losses. To mitigate these risks, it's important to set stop-loss orders and regularly re-evaluate the stocks in your portfolio.

Despite the risks, riding the trends has been a successful investment strategy for many investors over the years. Some of the most successful investors, such as Warren Buffett and Peter Lynch, have used this approach to generate significant returns in the stock market.

One strategy for riding the trends is to focus on industry trends. By identifying industries that are expected to grow or experience increased demand, investors can look for stocks in those industries that are likely to benefit. For example, investors who believe that the renewable energy sector is poised for growth might invest in companies that produce solar panels, wind turbines, or other renewable energy technologies.

Another strategy for riding the trends is to focus on company-specific trends. This involves identifying companies that are expected to benefit from specific events or trends, such as a new product launch or a major acquisition. For example, investors might invest in a company that is expected to benefit from the rollout of 5G technology or a company that has recently announced a partnership with a major retailer.

A third strategy for riding the trends is to use technical analysis to identify trends in stock prices. Technical analysis involves analyzing stock price charts and identifying patterns that suggest a stock is likely to continue to rise or fall. Investors who use technical analysis may look for stocks that are breaking out of a long-term trading range or stocks that are exhibiting a bullish or bearish trend.

One important parameter in technical analysis is price trends. Technical analysts study charts and graphs to identify patterns in price movements that may indicate a trend. For example, an uptrend occurs when prices move higher over time, while a downtrend occurs when prices move lower. Analysts may also look at support and resistance levels, which are price levels where the stock has previously had difficulty moving above or below.

Another important parameter in technical analysis is volume. Technical analysts believe that volume can provide insight into the strength of a trend. High volume during a price move suggests that a trend is likely to continue, while low volume may suggest that the trend is losing momentum. Volume can also be used to confirm or refute a price trend identified by other technical analysis indicators.

Moving averages are another important parameter in technical analysis. A moving average is a line that represents the average price of a security over a specified period of time. Technical analysts use moving averages to identify trends and determine support and resistance levels. For example, a 50-day moving average may be used to identify a short-term trend, while a 200-day moving average may be used to identify a long-term trend.

Investors who are looking to ride the trends in the stock market should also be prepared to adapt their strategies as market conditions change. This may involve selling stocks that are no longer benefiting from a trend or reallocating investments to take advantage of new trends. By staying informed and adaptable, investors can potentially ride the trends to maximize their returns and achieve their investment goals.

# CHAPTER 13.
# JIM SIMONS'
# QUANTITATIVE
# INVESTING APPROACH

Simons was born in Newton, Massachusetts, and grew up in Brookline, a suburb of Boston. His father was a shoe factory owner who encouraged his son's interest in mathematics from an early age. As a child, Simons enjoyed solving puzzles and reading books on mathematics and science. He attended the Massachusetts Institute of Technology (MIT) and earned a bachelor's degree in mathematics in 1958, followed by a Ph.D. in mathematics in 1962.

After completing his Ph.D., Simons worked as a research associate at MIT and as an assistant professor at Harvard University. He then joined the mathematics department at Stony Brook University in 1968, where he would spend the next thirty years. At Stony Brook, Simons became interested in geometry and topology, two areas of mathematics that would later prove useful in his work in finance.

His early work in mathematics focused on the study of geometric shapes and their properties. He made significant contributions to the field of differential geometry, which deals with the study of curves and surfaces. His work on the theory of minimal surfaces, which are surfaces that minimize their surface area, earned him international recognition in the mathematical community.

In the late 1970s, Simons became interested in the financial markets and began applying his mathematical skills to the analysis of market data. He founded a hedge fund, Monemetrics, in 1978, which used mathematical models to identify trends in the stock and commodity markets. However, the fund was not successful, and Simons shut it down in 1980.

Undeterred, Simons continued to refine his models and launched a new hedge fund, Renaissance Technologies, in 1982. He hired a team of mathematicians, computer scientists, and physicists to help him develop and implement his trading strategies. The fund initially focused on trading futures contracts, using computer models to analyze market data and identify patterns.

Renaissance Technologies' early years were rocky, and the fund struggled to generate consistent returns. However, Simons and his team persevered, and by the mid-1990s, the fund had become one of the most successful in the industry. Renaissance Technologies has consistently generated high returns for its investors, with its flagship Medallion Fund reportedly returning an average of 66% per year before fees between 1988 and 2018.

One of the key elements of Simons' investment approach is his focus on growth stocks. Simons looks for companies with strong fundamentals, such as high earnings growth rates, low debt-to-equity ratios, and strong cash flows. He also pays close attention to industry trends and emerging technologies, seeking out companies that are well-positioned to capitalize on new opportunities.

Jim Simons' investment approach is primarily based on quantitative analysis, which involves using mathematical models and statistical techniques to identify investment opportunities. Simons and his team of mathematicians and data scientists use complex algorithms and computer programs to analyze vast amounts of financial data in order to identify patterns and trends.

These models rely on a range of indicators and data points, including:

1. Price data: Renaissance's models analyze stock prices, including historical prices and current market trends, to identify patterns and trends.

2. Volume data: Trading volume is also an important indicator for Renaissance's models. High trading volumes can indicate buying or selling pressure and can help predict future price movements.

3. Market volatility: Renaissance's models analyze market volatility, which is the degree of variation in stock prices over time. High volatility can indicate greater risk, but it can also present profitable opportunities for skilled investors.

4. Economic data: Including GDP growth, inflation rates, and unemployment statistics, to help predict future market trends.

5. Fundamental data: Such as earnings reports, revenue growth, and profit margins, to assess the financial health and growth potential of individual companies.

6. News sentiment: Renaissance's models also analyze news sentiment and social media data to assess market sentiment and predict future trends.

One of the most famous stock investments made by Jim Simons was in the pharmaceutical company, Merck. In the late 1990s, Merck was facing a difficult time due to a series of high-profile drug recalls and lawsuits. The company's stock price was depressed, and many investors were shying away from it.

However, Simons saw an opportunity. He believed that the market had overreacted to the negative news and that Merck's long-term prospects were still strong. He decided to buy a large stake in the company, even as others were selling.

His bet on Merck turned out to be a wise one. The company's fortunes improved, and its stock price rose significantly. By the time he sold his stake in Merck in 2001, Simons had earned over $1 billion in profits. This was a remarkable return on investment, considering that he had only held the stock for a few years.

What made Simons' investment in Merck so successful? There are several factors to consider. First, Simons had a deep understanding of the pharmaceutical industry and the challenges that companies like Merck face. He knew that drug recalls and lawsuits were not uncommon and that they did not necessarily signal the end of a company's success.

Second, Simons was not swayed by short-term market fluctuations. He had a long-term perspective and was willing to hold onto a stock even during periods of volatility.

Finally, Simons had the discipline to stick to his strategy. He did not panic when others were selling Merck, and he did not get greedy when the stock price was rising. He sold his stake at the right time, based on his analysis of the company's prospects.

# CHAPTER 14.
# ANDREAS CLENOW'S QUANTITATIVE INVESTING APPROACH

Andreas Clenow is a prominent quantitative trader and author who has achieved significant success in the financial industry over the years. Clenow was born in Switzerland in 1972 and developed an early interest in finance and trading.

His first experience in the financial industry came in the early 1990s when he began working at a Swiss investment bank. He started out in a junior role but quickly moved up the ranks, eventually becoming a senior trader responsible for managing a significant portfolio of assets.

In the late 1990s, Clenow moved to London to work for a major investment bank. There, he continued to develop his skills as a quantitative trader and gained a reputation as an expert in systematic trading and portfolio management.

Starting his own hedge fund in the early 2000s, Clenow utilized his expertise in quantitative analysis and trading strategies to create a successful fund that produced strong returns for his investors. Over the years, Clenow continued to refine his approach to trading and investment management. He developed a systematic, quantitative approach that focused on identifying stocks with strong positive momentum and using a disciplined investment strategy to capitalize on these trends:

1. Market Trends: He pays close attention to market trends to identify stocks that are likely to perform well. He uses a variety of technical indicators to analyze trends and determine which stocks are likely to trend upwards.

2. Risk Management: Clenow places a strong emphasis on risk management when investing in stocks. He uses a variety of strategies to minimize risk, including diversification, stop-loss orders, and position sizing.

3. Fundamental Analysis: While he is primarily known for his quantitative analysis skills, he also pays attention to fundamental factors when making investment decisions. He considers factors such as earnings growth, dividend payouts, and valuation metrics to identify stocks that are likely to perform well over the long term.

4. Volatility: Clenow recognizes that volatility is an important factor when investing in stocks. He uses volatility-based indicators to determine the optimal entry and exit points for his trades, helping to minimize risk and maximize returns.

5. Backtesting: He uses backtesting to evaluate the performance of his trading strategies. He uses historical data to test his strategies and determine their effectiveness, helping him to refine his approach and identify new opportunities.

6. Automation: Clenow believes in the power of automation when it comes to investing in stocks. He uses automated trading systems to execute his

trades, helping to eliminate emotion and improve consistency.

7. Portfolio Optimization: He uses advanced mathematical models to optimize his portfolio and maximize returns while minimizing risk.

In addition to these indicators, Clenow also looks at a range of other factors when analyzing a stock, including its industry sector, its competitive position, and the overall market environment. He uses a combination of quantitative analysis and expert judgment to evaluate these factors and identify potential investment opportunities.

Clenow has also become a well-known author, publishing several books on systematic trading and investment strategies. His books, which include "Following the Trend" and "Stocks on the Move", are widely regarded as essential reading for anyone interested in quantitative trading and momentum investing.

He has achieved significant success in applying this approach to his trading. For example, he has reported earning returns of over 40% in some years by applying momentum investing strategies. This success has come from a combination of careful analysis of the markets and disciplined execution of his investment strategy.

In early 2017, Clenow made a significant investment in NVIDIA. His decision to invest in the company was based on several factors, including the growing demand for GPUs in various industries, such as gaming, artificial intelligence, and data center applications. NVIDIA is a leader in the GPU market and has a strong reputation for innovation and quality. Coupled with the company's solid financials, this made it an attractive investment opportunity for Clenow.

His investment in NVIDIA was also influenced by his investment philosophy, which emphasizes quantitative analysis and the use of trading systems. Clenow has developed a systematic approach to investing, which he calls "Swing Trading with a Twist". This approach involves using quantitative analysis to identify stocks that are likely to trend upwards and employing a set of trading rules to manage risk and maximize returns.

Clenow purchased NVIDIA stock at a price of $103 per share. Using his quantitative analysis and trading rules, he managed his position, which resulted in a strong return on his investment. The stock continued to trend upwards, reaching an all-time high of $615 per share in late 2020. This translates to an estimated gain of approximately 495% for Clenow on his investment in NVIDIA.

Another example of Clenow's success with momentum investing is his investment in the biotech company Biogen, which he purchased in 2010. At the time, Biogen was a relatively unknown company with a market capitalization of around $12 billion. However, Clenow saw potential in the company's strong pipeline of drugs and its focus on developing treatments for neurodegenerative diseases.

Clenow purchased Biogen at a price of around $54 per share, and held onto the investment for several years as the company's stock price continued to rise. In 2015, he sold the investment at a price of around $380 per share, earning a significant return on his initial investment.

# CHAPTER 15.
# DAVID HARDING'S QUANTITATIVE INVESTING APPROACH

David Harding was born on February 9th, 1961, in London, England. He grew up in a middle-class family and attended a comprehensive school in the London borough of Bromley. Harding was an intelligent student, and after finishing school, he went on to study physics at the University of Sussex.

After completing his degree, Harding began his career as a research scientist at Racal Electronics, a British electronics company. However, after a few years, Harding decided to pursue a career in finance and joined Bank of America as a financial analyst.

While working at Bank of America, Harding became interested in quantitative investing and started to develop his own trading algorithms. In 1990, Harding left Bank of America and co-founded AHL, a quantitative hedge fund, with two colleagues. AHL was one of the first hedge funds to use computer algorithms to make investment decisions.

Under Harding's leadership, AHL quickly became one of the most successful hedge funds in the world. By the late 1990s, the fund had grown to manage over $1 billion in assets and had delivered annualized returns of around 20%.

However, in 1997, Harding left AHL to start his own hedge fund, Winton Capital Management. Winton Capital Management initially started as a small operation with just a handful of employees, but it quickly grew into one of the most successful hedge funds in the world.

At Winton Capital, Harding continued to use quantitative investing strategies, including momentum investing, to achieve strong returns for his investors. He also developed new investment strategies, such as trend-following and statistical arbitrage, to further diversify the fund's portfolio.

Today, Winton Capital Management manages over $20 billion in assets and is one of the largest hedge funds in the world. Harding is widely regarded as one of the most successful quantitative investors of all time, and his pioneering work in the field of computerized trading algorithms has paved the way for a new generation of quantitative investors.

In 2007, Winton Capital made a substantial investment in Apple Inc., a technology company that was undergoing a transformation under the leadership of Steve Jobs, at a cost of around $12 per share. The investment turned out to be a profitable one for Winton Capital, and it was driven by several key factors.

Firstly, David Harding believed that Apple was a company with a strong brand and a loyal customer base. He recognized that Apple's products were in high demand, and that the company had a reputation for innovation and quality. He believed that Apple's products were so distinctive and well-designed that they would continue to attract consumers for years to come. This view was supported by Apple's financial performance at the time, which was strong and indicated a positive outlook for the future.

Secondly, Harding also recognized the potential of Apple's ecosystem. Apple had created a closed system that allowed it to control the hardware and software used in its products. This system allowed Apple to create a seamless and integrated user experience that was difficult for competitors to replicate. Harding believed that Apple's ecosystem would continue to attract and retain customers, and that this would translate into continued growth and profitability for the company.

Thirdly, Harding also took into account the broader technological and economic trends that were shaping the industry at the time. He recognized that the rise of mobile technology and the internet were creating new opportunities for companies like Apple. He saw that Apple was well-positioned to capitalize on these trends and to continue to innovate and grow.

Finally, Harding's investment in Apple was driven by a quantitative approach to investing. Winton Capital Management uses algorithms and data analysis to identify investment opportunities and make investment decisions. In the case of Apple, the firm used its quantitative models to analyze Apple's financial performance, market position, and other relevant factors. This approach allowed Winton Capital to make a well-informed investment decision based on objective data and analysis.

Over the next few years, Apple's stock price continued to rise, and by 2012, Winton Capital had sold its shares at a price of around $680 per share. This represents a significant return on investment for Winton Capital, with the shares increasing in value by over 5,500% over the five-year period.

David Harding used a variety of key indicators to analyze stocks and identify potential investment opportunities. These key indicators are based on mathematical models and statistical analysis and are used to identify stocks that are showing strong momentum or have the potential to generate strong returns.

One of the key indicators that Harding used is price momentum. Price momentum is a measure of the stock's recent price performance and is based on the idea that stocks that have shown strong price performance in the recent past are likely to continue performing well in the future. Harding would analyze a stock's price momentum by looking at the stock's price chart and identifying trends in the stock's price movement over time.

Another key indicator that Harding used is earnings momentum. Earnings momentum is a measure of a company's recent earnings performance and is based on the idea that companies that have shown strong earnings growth in the recent past are likely to continue growing their earnings in the future. Harding would analyze a company's earnings momentum by looking at the company's financial statements and analyzing trends in the company's revenue and earnings growth over time.

Harding also used technical indicators to analyze stocks. Technical indicators are based on mathematical formulas and are used to identify trends in a stock's price movement. Some of the technical indicators that Harding used include moving averages, relative strength index (RSI), and Bollinger Bands. Moving averages are used to smooth out a stock's price movement over time and identify trends in the stock's price movement. RSI is used to identify when a stock is overbought or oversold, and Bollinger Bands are used to identify when a stock's price is moving outside of its normal trading range.

In addition to these key indicators, Harding also used other quantitative analysis techniques, such as factor analysis and statistical arbitrage, to identify investment opportunities. Factor analysis involves identifying underlying factors that are driving stock prices, such as changes in interest rates or market volatility. Statistical arbitrage involves identifying pricing discrepancies between related securities and taking advantage of these discrepancies to generate profits.

Another example of how Harding applied momentum investing can be seen in his investment in Amazon.com Inc. In 2014, Winton Capital bought shares of Amazon at a cost of around $300 per share. At the time, Amazon was experiencing strong momentum due to the growth of its e-commerce business and the success of its Amazon Prime subscription service. Over the next few years, Amazon's stock price continued to rise, and by 2020, Winton Capital had sold its shares at a price of around $3,100 per share. This represents a significant return on investment for Winton Capital, with the shares increasing in value by over 1,000% over the six-year period.

# CHAPTER 16. MICHAEL MARCUS' TRADING APPROACH

Michael Marcus is widely known as one of the greatest traders of all time. He is a renowned trader and is famous for turning $30,000 into over $80 million in just 20 years.

He was born in 1945 in New York City and grew up in a family of modest means, and his father was a salesman. Marcus did not have a formal education in finance or trading, and he started his trading career as a commodities broker in the early 1970s. He worked at a brokerage firm where he learned about the commodities markets and trading.

Marcus was always interested in the financial markets, and he was an avid reader of financial publications. He became interested in trading after reading an article in Fortune magazine about a successful trader who had made a fortune trading soybeans. This inspired Marcus to pursue a career in trading.

In 1972, Marcus made his first trade in the commodities markets. He bought a soybean futures contract and made a small profit. This success gave him the confidence to continue trading. He began to study the markets and developed his own trading strategies.

His early trading days were not without their challenges. He lost money on several trades and had to borrow money from his mother to cover his losses. However, he was determined to succeed and continued to refine his trading strategies.

In the early 1980s, Marcus had his big break. He was introduced to legendary trader Ed Seykota, who mentored him and helped him develop his trading skills. Seykota taught Marcus about risk management, trend following, and the importance of discipline in trading.

Under Seykota's guidance, Marcus became a highly successful trader. He started his own trading firm and began trading for clients. He was one of the first traders to use technical analysis and trend following techniques in his trading. His trading philosophy was simple but effective. He believed that successful trading was a combination of three factors: a sound trading strategy, proper risk management, and the ability to execute trades with discipline. He also believed in the importance of constant learning and self-improvement.

One of Marcus's notable investments was in Berkshire Hathaway, the investment firm led by Warren Buffet. In the early 1980s, Marcus purchased Berkshire Hathaway shares for around $300 per share. He held onto the shares for several years, as the price steadily increased. Eventually, he sold his shares for over $1,000 per share, earning a significant profit. He recognized the upward trend in the price of the stock and capitalized on it.

As a momentum investor, Michael Marcus focused on analyzing a stock's price trends and movements in order to identify buying and selling opportunities. He believed that prices tended to continue to move in the same direction over a certain period of time, and that by identifying these trends, he could capitalize on them for profit. Some of the key indicators that Marcus used to analyze a stock included:

1. Moving Averages: Moving averages are used to smooth out fluctuations in a stock's price over

time. By looking at the stock's moving average over a certain period of time, Marcus could determine whether the stock was trending up or down.

2. Relative Strength Index (RSI): The RSI is a technical indicator that measures the strength of a stock's price movement. Marcus used this indicator to identify overbought and oversold conditions in a stock, which could signal a buying or selling opportunity.

3. Volume: Marcus also analyzed a stock's trading volume, as he believed that high trading volume indicated strong market interest in the stock. High volume could be a signal of a trend reversal or confirmation of an existing trend.

4. Price Patterns: He paid close attention to price patterns in the stock's chart, looking for patterns that indicated bullish or bearish sentiment. For example, a stock that forms a "head and shoulders" pattern could indicate a bearish reversal, while a "cup and handle" pattern could indicate a bullish continuation.

5. Market News: Marcus also considered market news and events that could affect the stock's price. This could include company earnings reports, economic data releases, or geopolitical events that could impact the stock's underlying fundamentals.

In the early 1980s, Michael Marcus made a bold move by investing heavily in Compaq Computer Corporation's stock, which was then a relatively unknown player in the computer industry. Marcus was a well-known commodities trader at the time and had a reputation for making successful trades based on his ability to identify trends in the market. However, his investment in Compaq was a departure from his typical approach to trading, which focused primarily on commodities.

Based on his analysis of the personal computer market, Michael Marcus invested in Compaq stock because he believed that the company had the potential to dominate this rapidly growing industry. Marcus saw that the company had a strong management team, a clear strategy for growth, and a commitment to innovation. He also believed that the company had a competitive advantage in the form of its ability to deliver high-quality products at a lower cost than its competitors.

His decision to invest in Compaq was also based on his analysis of the company's financials. He saw that the company had a strong balance sheet and was generating significant cash flows from its operations. He also believed that the company was undervalued by the market and that its stock price would rise as the company continued to grow and gain market share.

Another factor that influenced Marcus's decision to invest in Compaq was his experience as a trader. He had seen many companies come and go in the commodities market, and he recognized that Compaq had the potential to be a long-term winner. He also saw that the company's stock price was likely to be volatile in the short term, but he was willing to tolerate this volatility in order to achieve significant long-term gains.

Marcus's investment in Compaq turned out to be a prescient move. The company went on to become one of the dominant players in the personal computer industry, and its stock price soared in the years that followed. He purchased shares of Compaq at around $10 per share and held onto them as the price continued to increase. Eventually, he sold his shares for over $100 per share, earning a massive profit.

In the mid-1980s he invested in IBM stock, which was then considered a blue-chip company and a mainstay of the technology industry. Marcus paid around $100 per share for the stock, which was considered expensive at the time.

The rationale behind his investment in IBM was based on

his analysis of the company's financials, market position, and prospects for growth. He recognized that IBM had a strong balance sheet and was generating significant cash flows from its operations. He believed that the company's financial strength would help it weather any challenges that might arise in the future.

He was also impressed by IBM's market position as the dominant player in the computer industry. He saw that the company had a significant competitive advantage and believed that its strong brand and reputation would enable it to maintain its market position and continue to generate profits in the years to come.

In addition, Marcus recognized IBM's commitment to innovation. He saw that the company was investing heavily in research and development and was constantly introducing new products and services to the market. He believed that IBM's focus on innovation would enable it to stay ahead of its competitors and continue to grow in the years to come.

Finally, Marcus saw that IBM's stock price was undervalued by the market at the time. He believed that the company's potential for growth was not fully reflected in its stock price, and he saw significant upside potential in the stock.

Marcus's investment in IBM turned out to be a wise move. The company continued to dominate the computer industry, and its stock price rose significantly, generating substantial gains for Marcus. He held onto the stock for several years and sold it at a price of around $200 per share, earning a profit of around 100% on his investment.

In 1990, Marcus retired from trading at the age of 45. He had made a fortune from trading, and he wanted to spend more time with his family and pursue other interests. However, he continued to be involved in the financial industry and started a hedge fund in 1996.

# PART 5. BEHAVIORAL FINANCE AND RISK MANAGEMENT

*"The investor's chief problem - and even his worst enemy - is likely to be himself. In the world of money, the psychological effects of investment decisions are often more significant than the underlying economic factors. Fear, greed, and other emotions can lead investors to make irrational decisions, such as selling low or buying high. Understanding these behavioral biases is crucial to successful investing, as is having a solid risk management strategy. "*

*Benjamin Graham*

# CHAPTER 17. THE PSYCHOLOGY OF INVESTING

One of the most significant psychological biases that investors face is the fear of missing out (FOMO). FOMO can be described as the anxiety or apprehension that an investor feels when they believe that others are making profits in the market, and they are not. This fear can cause investors to make irrational decisions, such as buying high and selling low, in an attempt to catch up with others. To avoid FOMO, it is essential to have a clear investment strategy and stick to it, regardless of what others are doing in the market.

One of the most famous examples of this phenomenon occurred during the dot-com bubble of the late 1990s and early 2000s, when investors were caught up in the excitement of the new economy and the promise of internet riches. Kevin O'Connor, the founder and CEO of DoubleClick, an online advertising company that became one of the darlings of the dot-com boom, was a prominent investor of that era. O'Connor's visionary leadership had transformed DoubleClick into a billion-dollar company, cementing his reputation as an influential figure in the world of internet advertising.

However, despite his success, O'Connor couldn't resist the allure of the dot-com bubble. In 1999, he decided to invest $2 million of his own money in a start-up called TheGlobe.com. TheGlobe.com was an online community that allowed users to create their own web pages and connect with other users around the world. It was one of the hottest start-ups of the time, and its founders had just taken the company public in an IPO that was wildly oversubscribed.

O'Connor's investment in TheGlobe.com was a classic case of FOMO. He had missed out on the early stages of the dot-com boom, and he was determined not to miss out on the next big thing. He saw TheGlobe.com as a way to get in on the ground floor of a company that could be the next DoubleClick.

However, O'Connor's investment in TheGlobe.com turned out to be a disaster. The company's stock price soared in the weeks following its IPO, but it quickly came crashing down as investors realized that the company was not as profitable as they had hoped. O'Connor lost nearly all of his $2 million investment, and TheGlobe.com eventually went bankrupt.

Another common psychological bias is loss aversion, which is the tendency to avoid losses more than acquiring gains. Loss aversion can cause investors to hold on to losing investments for too long or sell winning investments too early. To avoid loss aversion, it is crucial to have a plan in place before investing, including setting clear stop-loss and take-profit levels. This will help investors to avoid making irrational decisions based on emotions.

One of the most famous examples of loss aversion in investing occurred during the financial crisis of 2008, when many investors were caught up in the panic and uncertainty of the market. Warren Buffett, the CEO of Berkshire Hathaway and a highly successful investor, was among the most prominent figures of that time. He had earned a reputation for his disciplined approach to investing, prioritizing long-term value over speculative bets. Nevertheless, Buffett demonstrated that even he was susceptible to the effects of loss aversion.

In 2008, Buffett made a major investment in the financial

services company Goldman Sachs. He saw the company as a solid bet that would weather the storm of the financial crisis and emerge stronger on the other side. However, as the crisis deepened, Goldman Sachs' stock price began to plummet. Buffett's investment was quickly losing value, and he faced a difficult decision: sell the stock and cut his losses, or hold on in the hope that the situation would improve.

Buffett's decision to hold on to his investment in Goldman Sachs was a classic example of loss aversion. He was unwilling to realize the loss and accept that his investment thesis had been wrong. Instead, he held on to the stock, hoping that the market would turn around and his investment would recover.

In the end, Buffett's bet on Goldman Sachs paid off. The company weathered the storm of the financial crisis and emerged as one of the strongest players in the financial services industry. Buffett's investment eventually recovered, and he made a substantial profit.

However, the story of Buffett and Goldman Sachs is a reminder of the dangers of loss aversion in investing. Investors who are unwilling to accept losses and cut their losses risk holding on to losing investments for too long, which can lead to even greater losses. While it's important to have confidence in one's investment thesis and to stick to a long-term strategy, it's equally important to be willing to accept losses and move on when a bet doesn't pan out.

Confirmation bias is another psychological bias that can affect investors. This bias refers to the tendency to seek out information that confirms pre-existing beliefs and ignore information that contradicts those beliefs. Confirmation bias can cause investors to overlook red flags or warning signs, leading to poor investment decisions. To avoid confirmation bias, investors should seek out information from a variety of sources and consider all the available information before making an investment decision.

In the early 2000s, a hedge fund manager named John Paulson became famous for making a fortune by betting against the housing market. Paulson was convinced that the housing market was overvalued and due for a collapse, and he built a large portfolio of bets against mortgage-backed securities and other housing-related assets.

Paulson's success was driven in part by his ability to recognize the signs of a housing bubble, but it was also fueled by his confirmation bias. As he researched the housing market and analyzed the data, he became increasingly convinced that a collapse was imminent. He sought out information that confirmed his beliefs and ignored information that contradicted them, such as rising home prices and strong economic indicators.

In the end, Paulson's confirmation bias paid off, and he earned billions of dollars for himself and his investors. However, his success also highlighted the dangers of confirmation bias in investing. Had the housing market not collapsed as he predicted, Paulson's portfolio would have suffered significant losses.

Overconfidence is another psychological bias that can lead investors astray. This bias refers to the tendency to overestimate one's ability to predict market movements and make successful investments. Overconfidence can lead to excessive risk-taking and the adoption of investment strategies that are too aggressive or complicated. To avoid overconfidence, investors should acknowledge the limitations of their knowledge and seek advice from professionals when necessary.

Finally, herd mentality is a psychological bias that can influence investment decisions. This bias refers to the tendency to follow the crowd and make investment decisions based on what others are doing, rather than on a well-thought-out strategy. Herd mentality can lead to irrational decision-making and significant losses. To avoid herd mentality, investors should have a clear investment strategy and stick to it, regardless of what others are doing in the market.

In the early 2000s, the United States was in the midst of a housing boom. Low interest rates and lax lending standards had made it easier than ever for Americans to buy homes, and many investors were eager to cash in on the boom. One of the most famous stocks of that era was Countrywide Financial, a mortgage lender that had become one of the largest companies in the country.

As the housing boom continued, Countrywide's stock soared. Investors were convinced that the company was an unstoppable juggernaut, and many poured their life savings into its shares. Analysts predicted that the stock would continue to rise indefinitely, and the company's CEO, Angelo Mozilo, became a household name.

However, not everyone was convinced. A handful of investors and analysts warned that Countrywide's lending practices were risky and unsustainable. They pointed out that the company was making loans to people with poor credit histories and that many of these loans were likely to default. They also noted that the housing market was becoming increasingly overheated, with prices rising far beyond the means of many buyers.

Despite these warnings, the herd mentality surrounding Countrywide's stock persisted. Investors continued to pour money into the company, driving its stock ever higher. The company's executives touted their success and brushed aside concerns about the risks of their lending practices.

In 2007, the housing bubble burst, and the risks that had been lurking beneath the surface of Countrywide's business model were exposed. The company was hit hard by the subprime mortgage crisis, and its stock plummeted. In 2008, Bank of America acquired Countrywide in a fire sale, and Mozilo was forced to resign in disgrace.

The psychology of investing is an essential aspect of successful investing. Investors must be aware of the various psychological biases that can influence investment decisions and take steps to avoid common pitfalls.

# CHAPTER 18.
# NAVIGATING BULL
# AND BEAR MARKETS

One of the most important factors to consider when navigating bull and bear markets is the overall economic climate. Economic factors such as inflation, interest rates, and gross domestic product (GDP) can have a significant impact on investment performance. For example, high inflation rates can erode the value of investments, while low-interest rates can make investments more attractive. In a bull market, the economy is typically growing, and investors are optimistic about the future, while in a bear market, the economy is usually contracting, and investors are more pessimistic.

Another crucial factor to consider is the overall trend of the market. Investors should pay attention to market indicators such as moving averages and trend lines to identify trends and potential reversals. Technical analysis can also be helpful in identifying patterns and signals that can indicate when to buy or sell investments.

In addition to economic factors and market trends, investors should also pay attention to the performance of individual stocks and sectors. In a bull market, investors tend to focus on growth stocks and high-risk sectors, while in a bear market, investors tend to focus on defensive stocks and sectors. By diversifying their portfolio across various sectors and asset classes, investors can minimize the impact of market volatility and reduce their risk exposure.

One of the most significant bull markets in history occurred in the 1990s. The period from 1990 to 2000 was characterized by strong economic growth, low inflation, and high corporate profits, which led to a surge in stock prices. The S&P 500 index rose from around 350 in 1990 to over 1,500 by the end of 1999, a gain of over 400%. This period is sometimes referred to as the "dot-com bubble," as many technology companies experienced explosive growth during this time.

However, the bull market of the 1990s was followed by one of the most significant bear markets in history. The period from 2000 to 2002 was characterized by a sharp decline in stock prices, as investors realized that many of the technology companies they had invested in were not profitable. The S&P 500 index fell from over 1,500 in early 2000 to around 800 by the end of 2002, a decline of nearly 50%.

Another example of a bull market occurred in the 1980s. The period from 1982 to 1987 was characterized by strong economic growth and low inflation, which led to a surge in stock prices. The S&P 500 index rose from around 100 in 1982 to over 330 by the end of 1987, a gain of over 200%.

However, the bull market of the 1980s was followed by a sharp decline in stock prices. The period from 1987 to 1990 was characterized by a series of market crashes, including the infamous Black Monday crash of October 19, 1987. The S&P 500 index fell from over 330 in August 1987 to around 230 by the end of 1987, a decline of nearly 30%.

One of the most prolonged bull markets in history occurred in the 1950s and 1960s. The period from 1949 to 1968 was characterized by strong economic growth and low inflation, which led to a surge in stock prices. The S&P 500 index rose from around 16 in 1949 to over 100 by the end of 1968, a gain of over

500%.

However, the bull market of the 1950s and 1960s was followed by a period of market volatility in the 1970s. The period from 1969 to 1982 was characterized by high inflation and stagnant economic growth, which led to a decline in stock prices. The S&P 500 index fell from over 100 in 1968 to around 100 by the end of 1982, a decline of nearly 50%.

Bull and bear markets have been a part of the financial world for many years. While bull markets are characterized by rising stock prices and strong economic growth, bear markets are characterized by falling stock prices and economic contraction.

# CHAPTER 19. BUILDING A DIVERSIFIED PORTFOLIO AND MANAGING RISK

Building a diversified portfolio is an essential strategy for managing risk and maximizing returns in the stock market. Diversification involves investing in a variety of different asset classes and sectors, rather than putting all of your money into a single stock or asset. This can help reduce the overall risk of your portfolio and minimize the impact of any individual stock's performance on your returns.

Here are some steps to building a diversified portfolio and managing risk:

1. Determine your investment goals and risk tolerance: Before investing, it's important to consider your investment goals and risk tolerance. This will help you determine the types of assets you should invest in and how much risk you are willing to take on.

2. Invest in a variety of asset classes: Diversifying your portfolio means investing in a variety of asset classes,

such as stocks, bonds, real estate, and commodities. Each asset class has different risks and returns, so investing in a mix of them can help balance out your portfolio.

3. Invest in a variety of sectors: Within each asset class, there are different sectors, such as technology, healthcare, and energy. Investing in a variety of sectors can help further diversify your portfolio and reduce the impact of any one sector's performance on your returns.

4. Consider index funds or exchange-traded funds (ETFs): Index funds and ETFs are investment vehicles that track a specific index or market segment. They offer exposure to a diversified portfolio of stocks or other assets, making them an easy way to build a diversified portfolio.

5. Rebalance your portfolio regularly: Over time, your portfolio may become unbalanced as some assets outperform others. Rebalancing involves selling some of the assets that have done well and reinvesting in those that have not performed as well. This helps keep your portfolio in line with your original asset allocation and risk tolerance.

6. Manage risk: While diversification can help manage risk, it's important to also consider other risk management strategies. This may include using stop-loss orders, which automatically sell a stock if it drops below a certain price, or using options contracts to hedge against potential losses.

By investing in a variety of asset classes and sectors, using index funds or ETFs, rebalancing your portfolio regularly, and considering other risk management strategies, you can build a portfolio that is better positioned to weather market fluctuations and deliver long-term returns.

# PART 6. INVESTING LEGENDS AND THEIR STRATEGIES

*"The stock market is filled with individuals who know the price of everything, but the value of nothing. Investing legends, on the other hand, understand that the key to successful investing lies in identifying valuable companies and holding on to them for the long-term. They know that investing is not a sprint, but a marathon, and that patience and discipline are essential to achieving their goals."*

*Peter Lynch*

# CHAPTER 20. WARREN BUFFETT'S VALUE INVESTING APPROACH

Buffett was born in 1930 in Omaha, Nebraska. He grew up in a middle-class family, and his father was a stockbroker and investor. Buffett showed an early aptitude for business and investing and began his first business at the age of six, selling chewing gum door-to-door. He attended the University of Nebraska and later transferred to the University of Pennsylvania, where he earned a degree in economics. While at Penn, Buffett studied under Benjamin Graham, who would later become a mentor and friend. Graham's value investing philosophy would influence Buffett's investment strategy for the rest of his life.

After graduating from Penn, Buffett briefly worked as a stockbroker, but he found the work unfulfilling and decided to strike out on his own. He started a partnership with several investors and began investing in stocks using Graham's value investing principles. The partnership was successful, and Buffett's reputation as a savvy investor began to grow.

In 1965, Buffett took control of the textile company Berkshire Hathaway and transformed it into an investment conglomerate. Under Buffett's leadership, Berkshire Hathaway invested in a wide range of companies, including insurance, retail, and manufacturing. Buffett's investment strategy was to buy companies that were undervalued by the market and hold them for the long term.

One of the key contributions that Buffett has made to the field of value investing is his emphasis on quality. He believes that in addition to buying stocks that are undervalued by the market, investors should focus on buying high-quality businesses with durable competitive advantages. This allows investors to benefit from the long-term growth potential of these businesses, as well as their ability to generate consistent earnings and cash flows.

In 1964, Warren Buffett made a significant investment in American Express, which at the time was dealing with a scandal involving its subsidiary, the salad oil company Allied Crude Vegetable Oil. The scandal had led to a sharp decline in American Express's stock price, making it an attractive investment opportunity for Buffett.

Buffett saw an opportunity in the market's overreaction to the scandal, and he believed that the strong brand and reputation of American Express would allow the company to recover. Buffett bought 5% of the company's stock for $13 million, making it one of his largest investments at the time.

His rationale for investing in American Express was based on his belief that the company had a unique competitive advantage due to its strong brand and customer loyalty. American Express was known for its high-quality customer service and its exclusive benefits, such as its charge card and travel services. Buffett believed that these qualities would allow American Express to continue to grow and generate profits over the long term.

Buffett's investment in American Express paid off, as the company's stock price recovered in the following years. By 1977, Buffett's initial investment had grown to $130 million, a tenfold increase in value. Today, Buffett's investment in American Express is worth over $20 billion, representing a remarkable return on his original investment.

Another significant contribution that Buffett has made is his emphasis on capital allocation. Buffett believes that the most important job of a CEO is to allocate capital in a way that generates the highest returns for shareholders. He has used his own success as an investor to influence the behavior of the companies he invests in, encouraging them to focus on long-term growth and sustainable profits.

Here are some key indicators that Warren Buffett uses to analyze a stock:

1. Earnings per share (EPS): He looks at a company's earnings per share over time, to determine if the company has a consistent track record of profitability. He looks for companies with a long history of steady earnings growth, rather than those with erratic or unpredictable earnings.

2. Return on equity (ROE): This measures how efficiently a company is using shareholder equity to generate profits. Buffett prefers companies with a high return on equity, as it shows that management is making effective use of shareholder funds.

3. Debt-to-equity ratio: Buffett generally prefers companies with low debt-to-equity ratios, as it reduces the risk of default and ensures that the company has more flexibility to invest in growth opportunities.

4. Free cash flow: This measures the amount of cash a company generates after accounting for capital expenditures. Buffett looks for companies that generate consistent free cash flow, as it provides the company with flexibility to reinvest in the business or pay dividends.

5. Management quality: He believes that strong

management is critical to the success of a company. He looks for companies with honest and competent management teams that have a track record of creating value for shareholders over the long-term.

In 1988, Warren Buffett made a significant investment in Coca-Cola, purchasing $1 billion worth of the company's stock. At the time, Coca-Cola was a dominant force in the soft drink industry, but its stock had been underperforming due to concerns about changing consumer preferences and increased competition.

Buffett saw an opportunity to invest in a company with a strong brand and a long history of success. He believed that Coca-Cola's brand was so strong that even if the company faced some short-term challenges, it would ultimately recover and continue to grow.

His investment in Coca-Cola was based on his belief in the power of brands. He saw Coca-Cola as a company with a powerful brand that had a loyal customer base and a global reach. Buffett believed that Coca-Cola's brand would allow it to continue to generate profits over the long term.

Buffett's investment in Coca-Cola has paid off handsomely. The company's stock has performed well over the years, and today, Buffett's investment is worth over $20 billion, representing a significant return on his initial investment.

According to Buffett, the key to successful investing is to identify companies whose intrinsic value is greater than their market value, and then invest in those companies for the long-term. Here is a step-by-step process of how Warren Buffett calculates the intrinsic value of a stock:

1. Analyze the Business: The first step in Warren Buffett's process of determining the intrinsic value of a stock is to analyze the underlying business.

This involves evaluating the company's competitive position, its growth prospects, its management team, and its financial performance. Buffett looks for companies that have a strong competitive advantage, such as a unique product or service, a loyal customer base, or a cost advantage over competitors.

2. Estimate Future Earnings: Once Buffett has a good understanding of the business, he then estimates the company's future earnings potential. He uses a combination of historical financial data, industry trends, and other factors to predict the company's future earnings growth rate.

3. Determine Discount Rate: The next step in Buffett's process is to determine the discount rate. This is the rate at which future earnings are discounted back to their present value. Buffett typically uses the U.S. Treasury bond yield as a benchmark for the discount rate.

4. Calculate Present Value: Using the estimated future earnings and discount rate, Buffett then calculates the present value of the company's earnings stream. This involves taking the projected future earnings and discounting them back to their present value.

5. Consider Margin of Safety: Finally, Buffett considers the margin of safety. This is the difference between the estimated intrinsic value of the stock and its current market price. Buffett looks for companies that have a wide margin of safety, meaning that their intrinsic value is significantly higher than their current market price.

Another example of Buffett's success is his investment in the Washington Post Company. In 1973, he invested $10.6 million in the company, which was then struggling due to rising production costs and declining ad revenue. Buffett saw value in the Post's reputation as a trusted news source and its ownership of several valuable assets, including TV stations and other media properties. Over the years, the Post Company's stock price steadily increased, and by 2013, Buffett's investment was worth over $1.1 billion, a more than 100-fold increase.

Warren Buffett's success as an investor can largely be attributed to his application of value investing principles. By identifying undervalued companies with strong growth potential, he has been able to build a massive fortune and achieve some of the highest returns in the history of the stock market. His investments in Coca-Cola, American Express, and the Washington Post Company are just a few examples of his success with this approach, and they serve as a testament to the power of value investing when applied correctly.

# CHAPTER 21. PETER LYNCH'S GROWTH INVESTING APPROACH

Peter Lynch is a legendary investor who made a name for himself as the manager of the Fidelity Magellan Fund from 1977 to 1990. During his tenure, he achieved an average annual return of 29.2%, making him one of the most successful mutual fund managers of all time. However, before he became a household name in the investing world, Lynch had to work his way up from humble beginnings.

Lynch was born on January 19, 1944, in Newton, Massachusetts. He grew up in a middle-class family and attended Boston College, where he earned a degree in economics. After graduation, Lynch worked as a stockbroker for Fidelity Investments, where he started as an intern in 1966.

His early days at Fidelity were challenging. He was initially placed in the research department, where he struggled to find stocks that would perform well. However, he soon realized that he could gain valuable insights into the stock market by studying companies and industries in his everyday life.

For example, Lynch noticed that his wife was using L'eggs pantyhose, a product that was growing in popularity at the time. He researched the company that made L'eggs, Hanes, and discovered that it was undervalued. He bought shares of Hanes and made a substantial profit when the company's stock price rose.

This experience taught Lynch an important lesson: successful investing requires both a keen eye for opportunities and a willingness to do the necessary research. He continued to use this approach throughout his career, often finding investment opportunities by observing everyday life.

In 1977, Lynch was appointed as the manager of the Fidelity Magellan Fund, which had only $20 million in assets at the time. He quickly made a name for himself as a skilled stock picker and grew the fund's assets to $14 billion by the time he retired in 1990.

His investment philosophy was based on the idea of investing in companies with strong growth potential. He believed that by identifying companies with high earnings growth rates, he could invest in them at an early stage and reap the benefits of their success over the long term.

One of Lynch's most famous investments was in a company called Dunkin' Donuts. In the early 1980s, Dunkin' Donuts was a relatively small regional chain of donut shops based in New England. Lynch saw the potential for the company to expand nationally and invested in the company's stock. He purchased shares of Dunkin' Donuts for around $10 per share, and over the years, the stock price increased significantly, reaching as high as $75 per share in the 1990s.

Another example of Lynch's successful growth investing strategy was his investment in Wal-Mart. In the 1970s, Wal-Mart was a small regional retailer operating in the southern United States. Lynch recognized the company's potential to grow into a national retail giant and invested in the company's stock. He purchased shares of Wal-Mart for around $3 per share, and over the years, the stock price increased significantly, reaching as high as $70 per share in the 1990s.

Lynch's investment in Amazon is also worth mentioning. In the mid-1990s, Amazon was a relatively unknown online bookstore. Lynch recognized the company's potential to disrupt the retail industry and invested in the company's stock. He purchased shares of Amazon for around $18 per share, and over the years, the stock price increased significantly, reaching as high as $3,500 per share in 2021.

It's important to note that Lynch's investment strategy wasn't just about identifying companies with strong growth potential. He also believed in doing thorough research and analysis before making an investment. He would spend hours reading financial statements, industry reports, and company news to gain a better understanding of the companies he was considering investing in. Here are some of the key indicators that Peter Lynch used to analyze a stock:

1. P/E Ratio: The price-to-earnings (P/E) ratio is a valuation metric that compares the current stock price with the earnings per share (EPS) of the company. Peter Lynch believed that a low P/E ratio could indicate an undervalued stock, while a high P/E ratio could indicate an overvalued stock.

2. EPS Growth: Peter Lynch also looked at the EPS growth rate to determine whether a company was growing its profits over time. He believed that a company with a consistently high EPS growth rate was likely to be a good investment.

3. Debt-to-Equity Ratio: The debt-to-equity ratio compares a company's total debt with its total equity. Peter Lynch preferred companies with a low debt-to-equity ratio, as it indicated that the company was not overly reliant on debt financing.

4. Dividend Yield: The dividend yield is the annual dividend paid by a company divided by the current

stock price. Peter Lynch believed that a high dividend yield could indicate a stable company that was returning value to its shareholders.

5. Price-to-Book Ratio: The price-to-book (P/B) ratio compares a company's stock price with its book value per share. Peter Lynch preferred companies with a low P/B ratio, as it indicated that the stock was undervalued relative to its book value.

6. Return on Equity: Return on equity (ROE) is a measure of a company's profitability that compares its net income to its shareholder equity. Peter Lynch preferred companies with a high ROE, as it indicated that the company was generating strong profits relative to its equity.

Lynch also had a long-term approach to investing. He believed in holding onto his investments for years, even if the stock price experienced short-term volatility. This approach allowed him to reap the benefits of the companies' growth over time and avoid the temptation to sell his shares too early.

However, it's worth noting that Lynch wasn't always investing in companies with high share prices. For example, as mentioned earlier, he purchased shares of Wal-Mart for around $3 per share in the 1970s. This demonstrates that Lynch wasn't solely focused on investing in high-priced stocks, but rather on identifying companies with strong growth potential.

# CHAPTER 22. GEORGE SOROS' TRADING APPROACH

George Soros is a well-known billionaire investor, philanthropist, and political activist. He was born on August 12, 1930, in Budapest, Hungary, to a Jewish family. Soros is famous for his investment strategies, political activism, and philanthropy, but his early life was marked by tragedy and upheaval.

Soros' family was relatively well-off before World War II. However, their fortunes took a turn for the worse when Hungary came under Nazi occupation in 1944. Soros, who was only 14 at the time, was forced to go into hiding and use false identity papers to avoid being captured by the Nazis. He witnessed first-hand the persecution of Jews and other minorities during the war, which had a profound impact on his worldview.

After the war, Soros moved to England to attend the London School of Economics. He worked odd jobs to support himself, including as a railway porter and a waiter, while studying philosophy and economics. It was during this time that Soros was exposed to the works of philosopher Karl Popper, who had a significant influence on his thinking. Popper's ideas about the fallibility of human knowledge and the importance of open societies would become central to Soros' worldview and activism.

After graduating from the London School of Economics, Soros

worked as a trader at various firms in London and New York City. He eventually founded his own hedge fund, Soros Fund Management, in 1973, which would make him one of the wealthiest people in the world.

His early investment strategies were heavily influenced by his experience of living through the turmoil of World War II and the Cold War. He believed that markets were inherently unstable and prone to crises, and that it was important for investors to be aware of the social and political factors that could influence market outcomes. This led him to develop his theory of "reflexivity," which argued that financial markets could influence the underlying fundamentals of the economy, and vice versa.

One example of Soros' growth investing approach is his investment in Microsoft in the 1990s. In 1992, Soros purchased a significant stake in the company, which was still in its early stages of growth. He paid around $22 per share for his initial investment, and over the next few years, Microsoft's stock price soared as the company's products became increasingly popular. Soros held onto his investment for several years, and by the time he sold his shares in 2000, he had earned an estimated $1.1 billion in profits.

Here are some of the key indicators that George Soros used to analyze a stock:

1. Macro Trends: George Soros believes that macroeconomic factors such as interest rates, inflation, and geopolitical events have a significant impact on the performance of individual stocks. He pays close attention to these macro trends and uses them to inform his investment decisions.

2. Management: Soros believes that the quality of a company's management team is critical to its long-term success. He looks for companies with strong leadership that have a track record of making sound business decisions.

3. Competitive Advantage: Soros also looks for companies with a competitive advantage in their industry. This could be a proprietary technology, a strong brand, or other factors that give the company an edge over its competitors.

4. Valuation: Soros believes that a stock's valuation is important in determining its potential for long-term growth. He looks for stocks that are undervalued relative to their earnings growth potential, and avoids stocks that are overvalued.

5. Technical Analysis: Soros also uses technical analysis to identify trends in a stock's price movements. He looks at charts and other technical indicators to determine the stock's momentum and whether it is likely to continue to rise or fall in the short term.

6. Margin of Safety: Soros is a strong proponent of the margin of safety principle, which involves investing in stocks that have a large margin of safety between their current price and their intrinsic value. This helps to reduce the risk of losses in case the stock price falls.

One of Soros' most famous investments was his bet against the British pound in 1992. He believed that the British government's economic policies were unsustainable and that the pound was overvalued. In the months leading up to his investment, Soros began to build up a large position in shorting the pound, essentially betting that its value would decline.

His investment paid off on September 16, 1992, when the British government was forced to withdraw the pound from the European Exchange Rate Mechanism (ERM) due to the currency's devaluation. Soros' short position allowed him to make a profit of approximately $1 billion in a single day, earning him the nickname "The man who broke the Bank of England."

Soros' rationale for his investment was based on his belief that the British government was overvaluing the pound by keeping interest rates high in order to maintain the currency's value. He saw this policy as unsustainable in the long term, and he believed that the pound's true value was much lower than its current exchange rate.

To build his position, Soros borrowed large amounts of pounds and sold them on the foreign exchange markets, essentially betting that the currency would decline. As the value of the pound began to decline, Soros' profits began to increase. His investment was helped by other investors who began to sell the pound as well, further exacerbating the currency's decline.

The investment in the pound was controversial, with some accusing him of engaging in speculative currency trading that destabilized the British economy. However, Soros defended his actions, arguing that he was simply taking advantage of market inefficiencies and that his investment was a legitimate way to make money in the financial markets.

His growth investing approach has also led him to invest in emerging markets. In the 1990s, he recognized the potential of the Chinese market and invested heavily in Chinese stocks. He also invested in other emerging markets, such as India and Brazil. Soros' investments in these markets have been highly profitable, as many of these countries have experienced strong economic growth over the past few decades.

# CHAPTER 23. CARL ICAHN'S ACTIVIST INVESTING APPROACH

Carl Icahn is a well-known investor and businessman, who is widely recognized for his aggressive investing style and his ability to turn around struggling companies. He was born on February 16, 1936, in Queens, New York, to a Jewish family. Icahn's early life was marked by hard work and determination, as he strove to achieve success in the competitive world of finance.

After graduating from Princeton University in 1957, Icahn worked as a stockbroker on Wall Street for a number of years. In the early 1960s, he founded his own investment firm, Icahn & Co., which specialized in buying and selling undervalued companies. Icahn quickly gained a reputation as an aggressive investor, who was not afraid to take on large corporations and challenge their management.

Over the years, Icahn has made a name for himself as a corporate raider, taking over struggling companies and using his business acumen to turn them around. He has been involved in a number of high-profile battles with companies such as Texaco, RJR Nabisco, and Yahoo!, and has been known to use aggressive tactics such as proxy fights and hostile takeovers to get what he wants.

His investing style is based on his belief that companies are undervalued due to poor management or market conditions, and that he can use his expertise and leverage as a shareholder to effect positive change. He is also known for his long-term approach to investing, often holding onto his positions for years at a time.

One of Icahn's most famous takeover events was his acquisition of the airline TWA (Trans World Airlines) in the 1980s. Icahn believed that TWA was undervalued and that he could unlock value by restructuring the company and selling off some of its assets.

Icahn began his takeover bid by acquiring a significant stake in TWA's common stock, eventually owning over 90% of the company's shares. He then used his controlling interest to force a restructuring of the company, including the sale of some of its assets and the renegotiation of labor contracts.

His strategy was successful, and he was able to sell off some of TWA's assets, including its London routes and its computer reservation system. He also renegotiated labor contracts, which reduced labor costs and increased profitability. Eventually, Icahn sold TWA to American Airlines for a substantial profit.

One example of Icahn's growth investing approach is his investment in Netflix. In 2012, Icahn bought a 10% stake in Netflix for around $58 per share, at a total cost of $323 million. At the time, the company was still relatively young and untested, but Icahn saw the potential for strong growth and believed that the stock was undervalued.

As it turned out, Icahn's investment in Netflix was a savvy move. Over the next several years, Netflix's subscriber base continued to grow, as did its revenue and profits. The company expanded into new markets and developed a strong reputation for producing high-quality original content.

By 2015, Icahn had sold his entire stake in Netflix for a total of around $1.4 billion, netting a profit of around $1.1 billion in just three years. This represented a return on investment of around

335%.

Icahn's investment in Netflix demonstrates his ability to identify undervalued companies with strong growth potential and to capitalize on those opportunities. He saw something in Netflix that others did not, and his faith in the company paid off handsomely.

It's worth noting that Icahn's investment in Netflix was not without its risks. At the time he bought the stock, many investors were skeptical of Netflix's ability to compete in a crowded market and to continue growing its subscriber base. However, Icahn's contrarian approach to investing allowed him to see past the skepticism and to identify the potential for strong growth.

He also made a bold move in 2013 when he began investing in Apple Inc., one of the world's largest tech companies. At the time, Apple was in the midst of a major transition, with the company's stock price underperforming and its future prospects uncertain.

Icahn saw an opportunity to capitalize on Apple's undervaluation, and in August 2013, he announced that he had taken a significant stake in the company. Over the next several months, Icahn increased his stake in Apple to over $3 billion, making him one of the company's largest individual shareholders.

At the time, many investors were skeptical of Apple's ability to continue innovating and growing in the face of increasing competition from rivals like Samsung and Google. However, Icahn believed that Apple had a strong brand and a loyal customer base, and that the company was undervalued relative to its true potential.

His bet on Apple paid off in a big way. Over the next few years, Apple continued to release innovative new products and services, including the iPhone 6 and 6 Plus, the Apple Watch, and the Apple Music streaming service. The company's revenue and profits soared, and its stock price rose steadily.

By the time Icahn sold his stake in Apple in 2016, he had earned a massive profit. He had bought his initial stake in Apple for around $68 per share, and over the course of his investment, the stock price had risen to around $110 per share. In total, Icahn's investment in Apple had earned him around $2 billion in profits.

His growth investing approach has also led him to invest in the technology and energy sectors. In the early 2000s, he recognized the potential of the technology sector and invested heavily in companies such as Yahoo! and eBay. He also invested in the energy sector, acquiring a significant stake in Chesapeake Energy in 2010. Icahn's investments in these sectors have been highly profitable, as many of these companies have experienced strong growth over the past few decades.

# CHAPTER 24. JOHN TEMPLETON'S GLOBAL INVESTING APPROACH

John Marks Templeton was born on November 29, 1912, in the small town of Winchester, Tennessee. His father, Harvey Templeton, was a successful lawyer and judge, while his mother, Birdie, was a devoted homemaker. John was the second of four children in the family. His parents instilled in him the values of hard work, thrift, and perseverance from an early age. These values would serve him well in his later life.

His early education was in the local schools of Winchester, Tennessee. He was an excellent student and had a keen interest in science and mathematics. He graduated from high school at the age of 16 and went on to attend Yale University. At Yale, he studied economics and graduated with honors in 1934.

After graduating from Yale, Templeton worked briefly for the National Bank of Commerce in New York City. However, he soon realized that he was more interested in pursuing a career in finance. In 1937, he enrolled in the Harvard Business School, where he earned his MBA. While at Harvard, he also worked part-time as a stockbroker, gaining valuable experience in the financial markets.

Upon finishing his MBA, Templeton went to work for the Wall Street investment firm, Fenner & Beane. There, he quickly distinguished himself as a shrewd investor, earning the nickname "The Boy Wonder" for his uncanny ability to pick winning stocks. In 1939, he left Fenner & Beane to start his own investment firm, the Templeton Growth Fund.

The early years of the Templeton Growth Fund were not easy. Templeton had to work hard to attract investors to his fledgling firm. He often traveled around the country, giving speeches and promoting his investment philosophy. However, his hard work paid off, and the Templeton Growth Fund soon became one of the most successful investment firms in the world.

One of his most successful investments was in Japan in the 1960s, where he saw an opportunity to invest in a market that was largely ignored by other investors. At the time, Japan was still recovering from the devastation of World War II, and its economy was relatively small and undeveloped. However, Templeton recognized the potential for strong growth in the Japanese market and began to invest heavily in Japanese stocks. His most successful investment in Japan was in the electronics company Fujitsu. In the early 1960s, Fujitsu was a relatively small company that was largely unknown outside of Japan. However, Templeton saw the potential for strong growth in the company and began buying shares.

At the time, Fujitsu was trading at just 2 times earnings, which was significantly lower than the valuations of other companies in the Japanese market. Templeton recognized that the market was undervaluing Fujitsu and saw an opportunity to generate significant returns by investing in the company.

Through a savvy investment in Fujitsu, one of Japan's largest electronics manufacturers by the mid-1960s, significant returns were generated for Templeton's clients as the value of the company's stock soared. Templeton's early investment in the company was a key factor in this success.

Another successful investment that Templeton made in Japan

was in the pharmaceutical company Yamanouchi. At the time, Yamanouchi was a relatively small company that was largely ignored by other investors. However, Templeton recognized the potential for strong growth in the company and began buying shares.

His investment in Yamanouchi paid off handsomely as well. By the early 1970s, the company had become one of the largest pharmaceutical companies in Japan, and its stock had skyrocketed in value. Templeton's early investment in Yamanouchi allowed him to generate significant returns for his clients.

Templeton's success as a growth investor extended to his investment in the emerging markets, where he recognized the potential for strong growth in developing countries like India and Brazil and made significant investments in companies operating in these markets. His contrarian approach once again proved fruitful, resulting in strong returns for his clients.

He was also known for his ability to identify long-term trends and invest in companies that were well-positioned to benefit from these trends. For example, he recognized the potential of the technology sector in the 1980s and invested heavily in companies such as Intel and Microsoft. His investments in these companies paid off handsomely, and he was able to generate significant returns for his clients.

# CHAPTER 25.
# MOHNISH PABRAI'S VALUE INVESTING APPROACH

Mohnish Pabrai was born in Mumbai, India in 1964. His family was not wealthy, but they placed a strong emphasis on education and hard work. Pabrai's father was an electrical engineer who encouraged his children to pursue careers in science and engineering. Pabrai followed his father's advice and earned a degree in mechanical engineering from the Indian Institute of Technology.

After graduating from college, Pabrai moved to the United States to pursue his dream of starting a technology company. He worked as an engineer for several years, but he quickly realized that he lacked the necessary business skills to succeed in the highly competitive world of technology startups. Undaunted, Pabrai decided to shift his focus to the stock market.

His interest in the stock market was sparked by a chance encounter with a book called "The Intelligent Investor" by Benjamin Graham. The book introduced Pabrai to the concept of value investing. He was immediately drawn to the idea of value investing, and he began devouring books and articles on the subject. He was particularly inspired by the career of Warren

Buffett, one of the most successful value investors of all time. Pabrai admired Buffett's disciplined approach to investing, and he sought to emulate his methods.

Pabrai started his investment journey with just $15,000 in the early 1990s, which he divided between a few Indian stocks. His investment approach proved to be fruitful, and he earned impressive returns on his initial investments. His top holdings at the time included companies like Tata Chemicals, Himachal Futuristic Communications, and Praj Industries. Pabrai's investments in these companies earned him over 200% returns within a few years, a remarkable feat considering that he was just starting out as an investor.

As Pabrai's success grew, he expanded his investment portfolio to include stocks in other markets, including the United States. In 1994, Pabrai founded his own investment partnership, Pabrai Funds. The fund initially started with just $1 million in assets, but it quickly grew as Pabrai's reputation as a savvy investor spread. His investment strategy was based on a deep understanding of the companies he invested in, and he was not afraid to take contrarian positions when he believed the market was undervaluing a particular stock.

His success as an investor was not without its challenges. In 2007, he made a costly mistake by investing heavily in the housing market just before the financial crisis. Pabrai lost nearly half of his fund's value, but he refused to give up. Instead, he redoubled his efforts and focused on his core strengths as an investor.

One example of Pabrai's value investing approach was his investment in the Korean automaker, Hyundai Motor Company. In 2004, Pabrai purchased a substantial stake in the company for around $27 per share, a price that he believed was undervalued given the company's strong fundamentals and growth potential. Over the next several years, Pabrai held the stock as the company's earnings and share price continued to rise. Eventually, he sold his stake for around $85 per share, earning a substantial return on his investment.

Pabrai also invested in General Motors (GM) in 2013. At the time, GM was trading at a low P/E ratio of around 5, which Pabrai believed was undervalued given the company's strong fundamentals. Pabrai purchased GM stock for his fund and held it for several years, eventually selling it for a substantial profit as the stock price rose along with the company's earnings.

In 2014, Pabrai made a significant investment in Fiat Chrysler Automobiles (FCA), an Italian-American multinational corporation that designs, manufactures, and sells vehicles under brands such as Jeep, Ram, Dodge, and Alfa Romeo. Pabrai's investment in FCA was based on his analysis of the company's financials, the potential for growth in emerging markets, and the management team's focus on improving operational efficiency.

His investment in FCA was significant, with his investment firm, Pabrai Investment Funds, investing over $100 million in the company. Pabrai saw the potential for significant growth in emerging markets such as India, Brazil, and China, where demand for vehicles was expected to increase rapidly. He believed that FCA was well-positioned to capitalize on this growth with its strong brand portfolio and global distribution network.

Furthermore, Pabrai was impressed by FCA's management team, particularly CEO Sergio Marchionne, who had a proven track record of turning around struggling companies. Marchionne had successfully revived Fiat's fortunes in the early 2000s and had also overseen the merger between Fiat and Chrysler in 2014, creating FCA. Pabrai believed that Marchionne's leadership and focus on improving operational efficiency would lead to improved profitability for the company.

Pabrai's investment in FCA proved to be a wise decision, as the company's stock price increased by over 200% within two years of his investment. Pabrai's investment firm made a profit of over

$200 million on its investment in FCA, a significant return on investment.

However, Pabrai's success was not solely due to his investment philosophy. He also demonstrated great discipline and patience in his investment approach, refusing to make rash decisions and maintaining a long-term outlook. He stuck with his investments even during periods of volatility, knowing that they would eventually yield positive returns in the long run.

# CHAPTER 26. JOEL GREENBLATT'S VALUE INVESTING APPROACH

Greenblatt was born in 1957 in Great Neck, New York, and grew up in a middle-class family. His father was a lawyer, and his mother was a homemaker. Greenblatt showed an early aptitude for academics and was accepted into the prestigious Bronx High School of Science. After graduating, he went on to attend the University of Pennsylvania, where he earned a degree in economics.

While at Penn, Greenblatt became interested in investing and spent much of his free time studying the stock market. He read books, attended investment conferences, and began trading stocks with a small amount of money he had saved up. Greenblatt's early forays into investing were not always successful, but he persisted and continued to learn from his mistakes.

After graduating from Penn, Greenblatt went on to earn an MBA from the Wharton School. He then worked for several years as a consultant at the management consulting firm McKinsey & Company. However, he found the work unfulfilling and decided to leave the firm to focus on investing full-time.

Greenblatt's first investment venture was a hedge fund he started in the late 1980s called Gotham Capital. The fund was initially funded with just $7 million in assets, but it quickly grew as Greenblatt's reputation as a savvy investor spread. Gotham Capital was known for its contrarian investment strategies, which involved buying stocks that were undervalued by the market and shorting those that were overvalued.

His investment strategy proved highly successful, and Gotham Capital consistently generated returns that were far above average. One of the fund's most successful investments was in the stock of a bankrupt steel company called National Can, which Greenblatt bought for just $0.50 per share. Over the course of several years, the stock eventually rose to over $30 per share, earning Gotham Capital a massive return on its investment.

In addition to his work at Gotham Capital, Greenblatt is also known for his book "The Little Book That Beats the Market", which outlines his investment strategy in easy-to-understand terms. The book has become a classic in the world of finance and has been widely praised for its clear and concise explanation of value investing. He believes in identifying undervalued companies with strong earnings yields and high returns on capital, and he has been able to generate significant returns using this approach.

Here's how to use his "Magic Formula":

1. Identify a universe of stocks: Start by identifying a universe of stocks that you're interested in. This can be all stocks traded in a specific market or sector.

2. Calculate the earnings yield: To calculate the earnings yield of a stock, divide its earnings per share (EPS) by its price per share (P/E ratio). For example, if a stock has an EPS of $5 and a P/E ratio of 10, its earnings yield would be 50%.

3. Calculate the return on capital: To calculate the return on capital of a stock, divide its earnings before interest and taxes (EBIT) by its net working capital

plus net fixed assets. This will give you a percentage that represents the company's return on the capital it has invested.

4. Rank stocks: Once you have calculated the earnings yield and return on capital for each stock in your universe, rank them based on their combined score. To do this, add the earnings yield and return on capital percentages together for each stock.

5. Invest in top-ranked stocks: Invest in the top-ranked stocks based on your ranking system. You can choose the top 10%, 20%, or any other percentage that you prefer.

It's worth noting that the Magic Formula is designed as a long-term investment strategy, and Greenblatt recommends holding the top-ranked stocks for at least a year. Additionally, it's important to conduct thorough research on each stock before investing, as the Magic Formula alone does not guarantee success.

One example of Greenblatt's success with value investing is his investment in retailer AutoZone. In the late 1990s, AutoZone was a struggling company with declining sales and a tarnished reputation. However, Greenblatt saw value in the company's strong brand, its dominant market position, and its ability to generate significant cash flows. He invested heavily in the company, and over time, his investment generated significant returns. As of 2021, his investment in AutoZone was worth over $3 billion, a more than fiftyfold increase.

An investment that proved highly successful for him was made in Progressive Corporation, an insurance company specializing in automobile insurance for US customers. Greenblatt arrived at this investment decision by carefully scrutinizing the company's financial statements and assessing its competitive position in the insurance sector. His analysis led him to believe that Progressive enjoyed a sustainable competitive advantage, thanks to its sophisticated use of technology and data analysis in underwriting policies. This, in turn, enabled the company to price its policies more precisely and expertly manage risk.

In addition, Greenblatt was attracted to Progressive's strong financial performance, which was reflected in its high return on equity (ROE) and consistent earnings growth. He also noted that the company had a relatively low valuation compared to other insurance companies in the industry, which he saw as an opportunity to purchase the stock at a discounted price.

His investment in Progressive Corporation was made in the mid-1990s, when the company was still a relatively small player in the insurance industry. He purchased the stock for around $2 per share, which was considered a bargain at the time given the company's strong financials and growth potential.

Over the next few years, Progressive's stock price increased significantly, driven by the company's continued growth and success in the insurance market. By the early 2000s, the stock was trading at around $30 per share, representing a substantial increase from Greenblatt's initial investment.

Greenblatt has also found success with investments in smaller companies. In the mid-2000s, he invested in the pharmaceutical company Allergan, which was then trading at a significant discount to its intrinsic value. Greenblatt saw value in Allergan's strong pipeline of products, its leading market position, and its ability to generate significant cash flows. He invested heavily in the company, and over time, his investment generated significant returns. As of 2021, his investment in Allergan was worth over $1 billion, a more than tenfold increase.

# CHAPTER 27. ED SEYKOTA'S TRADING APPROACH

Ed Seykota, born in 1946, is a renowned trader who is widely recognized for his contribution to the development of trend following and technical analysis. Seykota's early days were marked by his passion for mathematics and interest in the stock market, which ultimately led him to become one of the most successful traders of his time.

His fascination with the stock market began during his teenage years when he became interested in reading financial newspapers and analyzing the stock market. This led him to pursue a degree in Electrical Engineering at MIT, where he was exposed to the principles of probability theory and statistics, which helped him develop a quantitative approach to trading.

After completing his degree, Seykota began his career as an analyst at a brokerage firm in Chicago. It was during this time that he discovered the work of Richard Donchian, a pioneer in the field of trend following. Donchian's approach to trading was based on the idea that markets trend and that traders can make profits by identifying and riding these trends.

Seykota was fascinated by Donchian's approach and decided to develop his own trading system based on these principles. He began testing his system on historical data and soon found that it was highly effective in identifying trends and making profitable trades.

His trading system relied heavily on technical analysis, which involves studying price charts and other market data to identify trends and patterns. He used a variety of technical indicators, such as moving averages, to help him identify trends and determine when to enter or exit trades.

In the early 1970s, Seykota moved to California and became a member of the newly formed Commodities Corporation, which was founded by two legendary traders, Richard Dennis and Bill Eckhardt. At Commodities Corporation, Seykota was able to refine his trading system and develop new techniques for identifying trends and managing risk.

Seykota's trading success at Commodities Corporation soon caught the attention of other traders and investors, and he began managing money for outside clients. His track record of consistently delivering high returns on investment earned him a reputation as one of the best traders in the business.

One example of Seykota's success with momentum investing is his investment in the stock of a company called MCI. In the early 1980s, MCI was a telecommunications company that was challenging AT&T's monopoly in the US. Seykota saw that the stock of MCI had been showing a steady upward trend in price, and decided to invest in it. He bought the stock at around $6 per share, and held onto it as it continued to rise in price. Eventually, he sold his shares for around $90 per share, making a profit of more than 1,400%.

Seykota used a variety of technical indicators to analyze stocks and determine when to enter or exit trades. Some of the key indicators he used include:

1. Moving Averages: A trend-following indicator that helps traders identify the direction of the trend.

Seykota used moving averages to identify support and resistance levels, as well as to determine when a trend was likely to reverse.

2. Relative Strength Index (RSI): The RSI is a momentum indicator that measures the strength of a stock's price action. Seykota used the RSI to identify overbought and oversold conditions in a stock, which can help traders determine when to enter or exit a trade.

3. Bollinger Bands: A volatility indicator that helps traders identify periods of high and low volatility. Seykota used Bollinger Bands to identify when a stock was likely to break out of a trading range, which can provide a profitable trading opportunity.

4. Fibonacci Retracement: A technical analysis tool that helps traders identify potential levels of support and resistance. Seykota used Fibonacci retracement levels to identify potential entry and exit points for trades.

5. Price Action: Price action refers to the movement of a stock's price over time. Seykota used price action analysis to identify key levels of support and resistance, as well as to identify potential breakout or reversal patterns.

In addition to these technical indicators, Seykota also used fundamental analysis to evaluate the financial health and growth prospects of a company. This involved analyzing financial statements, industry trends, and other market data to determine whether a stock was undervalued or overvalued.

In the early 1990s he bought Amgen stock at around $15 per share and held onto it for several years, during which time the stock experienced significant growth. Seykota's investment in Amgen was based on several key factors.

Firstly, he recognized the emerging growth potential of the biotech industry, given the increasing demand for healthcare and the aging of the population. He believed that Amgen was well-positioned to capitalize on this trend.

Secondly, Seykota was impressed by Amgen's strong track record of innovation and product development. The company had a pipeline of new drugs and therapies in development, and Seykota believed that these products had the potential to be highly successful in the market.

Thirdly, Seykota was impressed by Amgen's financial performance. The company had a solid balance sheet and was consistently profitable, with strong cash flows and a low debt-to-equity ratio. He believed that these financial metrics were a good indicator of the company's long-term viability and growth potential.

Finally, Seykota recognized that Amgen was a leader in its industry and had a strong competitive advantage. The company's products were highly regarded by healthcare professionals and patients, and Amgen had established strong relationships with key players in the healthcare industry. Seykota believed that these factors would help to protect Amgen's market position and allow the company to continue to grow and expand over the long term.

His investment in Amgen turned out to be a wise decision, as the stock price soared over the years. He reportedly sold his Amgen shares for around $100 per share, earning a considerable profit.

# CHAPTER 28. THOMAS ROWE PRICE JR.'S GROWTH INVESTING APPROACH

Thomas Rowe Price Jr was an American investor and founder of the T. Rowe Price investment management firm. Born on February 16, 1898, in Linwood, Maryland, Price grew up in a family of farmers. He was the third child and only son of Florence Rowe and Thomas Rowe Price Sr. Price's father was a successful tobacco farmer, and his mother was a teacher.

He was a bright student and graduated from Swarthmore College in Pennsylvania with a degree in chemistry. After college, he worked briefly as a chemist but soon realized that his true passion was in finance. He went on to study accounting and finance at the Johns Hopkins University.

In 1919, Price began his career at the investment firm of Mackubin, Goodrich & Co. in Baltimore. He quickly made a name for himself as a talented analyst and investor. His investment philosophy focused on finding undervalued companies with strong long-term growth prospects.

In 1937, Price left Mackubin, Goodrich & Co. to start his own investment firm, the T. Rowe Price Associates. He initially ran the firm out of his home with a staff of just four employees. However,

Price's reputation as a successful investor attracted a growing number of clients, and the firm soon expanded.

Throughout his career, Price was known for his disciplined approach to investing. He believed that successful investing required careful research and analysis, as well as a long-term perspective. He was also a strong believer in diversification, encouraging his clients to spread their investments across different industries and asset classes.

One example of Price's growth investing strategy is his investment in Xerox. In the 1960s Xerox was a relatively unknown company that was struggling to sell its high-priced copiers. However, Price saw potential in the company and believed that it could become a leader in the copier industry.

His investment in Xerox was based on his analysis of the company's potential for growth. He believed that Xerox had developed a superior technology and had a strong management team that could successfully market and sell their products. In addition, he saw that the company had a unique business model that allowed it to generate high profits from each copier sold, which he believed would lead to strong earnings growth in the future. Here are some of the key indicators that he used when investing in stocks:

1. Revenue Growth: Price looked for companies with a strong track record of revenue growth. He believed that companies that were able to consistently increase their revenue were well-positioned to generate long-term earnings growth.

2. Earnings Growth: Price also looked for companies with a strong track record of earnings growth. He believed that companies that were able to consistently increase their earnings were well-positioned to deliver long-term value to investors.

3. Management Quality: Price placed a strong emphasis on the quality of a company's management team. He looked for companies with strong, visionary leaders who had a proven track record of success in their industry.

4. Competitive Advantage: Price also looked for companies with a strong competitive advantage. He believed that companies with a unique product or service that was difficult to replicate by competitors were well-positioned to generate long-term earnings growth.

5. Industry Trends: Price also paid close attention to industry trends and emerging technologies. He believed that companies that were able to stay ahead of the curve and adapt to changing market conditions were well-positioned to generate long-term earnings growth.

In the early 1980s, Thomas Rowe Price recognized the potential of the emerging personal computer industry and invested heavily in Intel. At the time, Intel was a relatively unknown company that produced microprocessors, which were the key components of personal computers.

Price's investment in Intel was a bold move, as the company was not yet widely recognized as a leader in the industry. However, Price saw the potential for growth in the emerging personal computer market and believed that Intel was well-positioned to capitalize on this trend. His investment in Intel paid off handsomely. Over the next few decades, Intel became a dominant player in the personal computer industry, and Price's investment in the company earned him significant profits. Intel's stock price grew from around $1.50 per share in the early 1980s to over $30 per share by the late 1990s.

# CHAPTER 29. JOHN W. HENRY'S TRADING APPROACH

John W. Henry was born on September 13, 1949, in Quincy, Illinois. He grew up in a middle-class family and attended Victor Valley High School in California. In his early years, Henry was interested in sports and played baseball and football in high school.

After graduating from high school, Henry attended Victor Valley College and later transferred to the University of California, Riverside, where he earned a degree in agriculture. However, Henry's interests shifted towards finance and investing, and he began reading books on the subject in his spare time.

In the early 1970s, Henry moved to Chicago and started his career as a commodities trader. He worked for various trading firms and gained experience in the futures markets. However, Henry struggled to make consistent profits and was eventually fired from his job.

Undeterred, Henry decided to start his own trading firm and founded John W. Henry & Company in 1981. The company initially focused on trading in the futures markets, using computer algorithms to identify trading opportunities. Henry's innovative use of technology and data analysis helped him gain an edge in the market and led to the firm's success.

In the late 1980s, Henry began applying the Momentum Investing strategy to his investments, buying and selling stocks based on their momentum. This strategy proved to be highly successful, and the firm's assets under management grew rapidly.

Henry recognized that Whirlpool, a manufacturer of home appliances such as refrigerators, washing machines, and dryers, was a well-established company with a strong brand reputation and a dominant market share in its industry. He also noted that the company was experiencing solid financial performance, with consistent revenue growth and strong profitability.

He purchased shares of Whirlpool Corporation in 2018 at an average price of $148.94 per share. As of 2021, the stock price had risen to over $240 per share, resulting in a total return of over 60% for Henry's investment.

In addition to his success in finance, Henry has also been involved in sports ownership. In 1991, he made the decision to purchase the Florida Marlins baseball team for a reported $95 million. At the time of Henry's purchase, the Marlins were a relatively new expansion team that had struggled to gain a foothold in the competitive baseball market. Despite their struggles, Henry saw the potential for the team to succeed and set out to build a winning franchise.

Henry brought a unique perspective to sports ownership, drawing on his experience as a successful investor and entrepreneur. He recognized that building a successful sports team required a similar approach to building a successful business - identifying key areas of strength, investing in talent, and strategically managing resources.

Under Henry's ownership, the Marlins began to experience significant success on the field. In 1997, the team won its first World Series championship, thanks in part to key acquisitions such as pitcher Kevin Brown and outfielder Moises Alou.

However, Henry's tenure as the owner of the Marlins was not without controversy. He clashed with local officials over plans to build a new stadium and faced criticism from fans for his decision to sell off key players following the team's championship win.

In 1999, Henry made the decision to sell the Marlins to a group of investors for a reported $158 million. While he had achieved his goal of building a winning franchise, Henry recognized that sports ownership was a challenging and unpredictable business.

John W. Henry and his investment group, New England Sports Ventures, made a notable sports ownership investment when they purchased the Boston Red Sox baseball team for $700 million. Henry saw the team as an undervalued asset with the potential for significant growth if managed correctly. Applying his Momentum Investing strategy, he believed that he could improve the team's performance on the field and increase its value off the field.

His strategy was to invest heavily in the team's roster, bringing in high-performing players who were in the prime of their careers. He also invested in the team's infrastructure, building a state-of-the-art training facility and upgrading Fenway Park, the team's historic home stadium. These investments paid off on the field, as the Red Sox won three World Series championships under Henry's ownership, in 2004, 2007, and 2013.

Off the field, Henry's investments in the team's infrastructure and marketing helped increase the team's revenue significantly. In 2002, the team's revenue was $162 million, but by 2010, it had grown to $302 million. This growth in revenue was driven by increases in ticket sales, merchandise sales, and sponsorships, which were all directly related to the team's success on the field.

In 2011, after nearly a decade of ownership, Henry decided to sell the Boston Red Sox. He believed that the team's value had peaked and that it was time to cash out his investment. In addition, he wanted to focus on his other business ventures, including his financial management firm, John W. Henry & Company.

Henry sold the team for $1.1 billion, which was a significant return on his initial investment of $700 million. This profit was largely driven by the team's success on the field and its growth in revenue off the field, which had increased the team's overall value.

One of his most notable sports ownership investments was his acquisition of Liverpool Football Club in 2010. At the time of the acquisition, John W. Henry's investment group, Fenway Sports Group, paid £300 million (approximately $477 million USD) for Liverpool Football Club. The purchase was made after the previous owners, Tom Hicks and George Gillett, defaulted on their loans, which led to a legal battle and the club being put up for sale.

His investment in Liverpool was based on his belief that the club was undervalued and had the potential for significant growth. He saw the club as a valuable asset with a rich history and a dedicated fan base, and he believed that with the right management and investment, the team could be successful both on and off the field.

Under Henry's ownership, Liverpool has experienced a significant transformation. The team has won several major trophies, including the UEFA Champions League, the Premier League, and the FIFA Club World Cup. In addition, the club has seen significant growth in its commercial revenue, with sponsorships and merchandise sales increasing.

As of 2023, Liverpool Football Club is valued at approximately £2.25 billion (approximately $2.83 billion USD), which is a significant increase from the £300 million that Henry paid for the club in 2010.

# PART 7. CONCLUSION

*"An investment in knowledge pays the best interest, but to earn interest, you must have a plan, and you must implement that plan."*

*T. Rowe Price*

# CHAPTER 30.
# DEVELOPING YOUR INVESTMENT PHILOSOPHY AND BUILDING A SUCCESSFUL INVESTMENT PLAN

Developing your own investment philosophy and building a successful investment plan can be a challenging task, but it is essential to achieving your financial goals. Here are some key steps in developing an investment philosophy and building a successful investment plan:

1. Define Your Investment Objectives: The first step in developing your investment philosophy is to define your investment objectives. This involves identifying your financial goals, such as retirement planning, wealth accumulation, or risk management. Once you have a clear understanding of your investment objectives, you can begin to develop an investment strategy that aligns with your goals.

2. Determine Your Risk Tolerance: This involves assessing your ability and willingness to tolerate investment risks. Your risk tolerance will depend on various factors, such as your age, financial situation, and investment experience. It is essential to understand your risk tolerance as it will impact the type of investments you make.

3. Select Your Investment Style: There are various investment styles, such as value investing, growth investing, and index investing. Each style has its own advantages and disadvantages, and it is essential to choose an investment style that aligns with your investment objectives and risk tolerance.

4. Build Your Investment Portfolio: Select the specific investments that will make up your portfolio, such as stocks, bonds, mutual funds, and exchange-traded funds (ETFs). It is essential to diversify your portfolio across different asset classes to minimize risk and maximize returns.

5. Monitor and Rebalance Your Portfolio: The final step in building a successful investment plan is to monitor and rebalance your portfolio regularly. This involves reviewing your investments regularly and making changes as necessary to ensure that your portfolio continues to align with your investment objectives and risk tolerance.

Rebalancing your investment portfolio is a critical aspect of maintaining a successful long-term investment strategy. Over time, the value of different assets in your portfolio will fluctuate, causing your original asset allocation to become unbalanced. Rebalancing involves selling some assets and buying others to restore your portfolio to its original allocation.

One of the primary benefits of rebalancing your portfolio is that it helps you maintain your target asset allocation. A well-diversified portfolio should include a mix of stocks, bonds, and other assets that align with your investment goals, risk tolerance, and time horizon. However, as the value of these assets fluctuates, your portfolio's allocation can become skewed, leading to unintended risks or lower returns. By rebalancing, you can ensure that your portfolio remains aligned with your investment strategy.

Another benefit of rebalancing is that it forces you to buy low and sell high. When one asset class outperforms others, its share of your portfolio will increase, leaving you with a higher risk profile than you intended. By selling some of those assets and buying others that have underperformed, you can take advantage of market fluctuations and potentially improve your long-term returns.

Greenblatt recommends that investors hold between 20 to 30 stocks in their portfolio. This is in contrast to the conventional wisdom that a diversified portfolio should contain at least 50 to 100 stocks. However, Greenblatt argues that the number of stocks in a portfolio is not as crucial as the quality of the stocks chosen. He believes that by investing in high-quality, undervalued companies, investors can build a diversified portfolio that is positioned for long-term growth.

His philosophy is based on the idea that the market can sometimes misprice stocks, creating opportunities for investors who are willing to look beyond short-term market trends and focus on a company's earnings potential. By investing in a small number of high-quality, undervalued companies, investors can potentially benefit from long-term growth and achieve diversification through exposure to different sectors and industries.

So when should you rebalance your portfolio? There are different approaches to determining when to rebalance, but a common rule of thumb is to rebalance when your asset allocation deviates from your target allocation by a certain percentage. For example, if your target allocation is 60% stocks and 40% bonds, you may choose to rebalance if stocks comprise 65% of your portfolio. However, it's important to consider the cost of rebalancing, such as transaction fees and taxes, and balance that against the potential benefits.

Once you've determined that it's time to rebalance, the next step is to execute your strategy. There are different approaches to rebalancing, but one common method is to sell assets that have overperformed and buy assets that have underperformed, effectively buying low and selling high. Another approach is to use new cash flows, such as dividends or contributions, to rebalance your portfolio rather than selling assets.

It's also important to consider the tax implications of rebalancing, particularly if you have investments in taxable accounts. Selling assets to rebalance can generate capital gains or losses, which can impact your tax liability. However, if you have losses in other areas of your portfolio, you may be able to offset those gains and potentially reduce your tax bill.

In conclusion, developing your own investment philosophy and building a successful investment plan requires careful consideration of your investment objectives, risk tolerance, investment style, and portfolio construction. By following these key steps, you can develop an investment plan that aligns with your goals and helps you achieve financial success. It is also essential to seek the advice of a financial advisor to help guide you through the investment process and provide valuable insights and expertise.

# ABOUT THE AUTHOR

**JACK FISHER** is a former engineer, entrepreneur, and investor. He lives in California, United States with his fiancé and two children. Jack loves educating and inspiring other investors and entrepreneurs to succeed and live the life of their dreams.

www.ingramcontent.com/pod-product-compliance
Lightning Source LLC
Chambersburg PA
CBHW070553220526
45467CB00003B/1202